THE BLUE PRINT TO SUCCESS

Bible-based success principles with practical applications for your everyday life!

Stacy D. Coward

iUniverse®

THE BLUE PRINT TO SUCCESS
BIBLE-BASED SUCCESS PRINCIPLES WITH PRACTICAL APPLICATIONS FOR YOUR EVERYDAY LIFE!

Author Credits: Robbie Rawls, Diana L. McDonald, John Earl McDonald, Arthur M. Jagers Jr, Charity F. Johnson, Ashley J. Robinson, Damon L. Robinson, Robin M. Dorkins

iUniverse books may be ordered through booksellers or by contacting:

iUniverse
1663 Liberty Drive
Bloomington, IN 47403
www.iuniverse.com
1-800-Authors (1-800-288-4677)

ISBN: 978-1-5320-3947-8 (sc)
ISBN: 978-1-5320-3948-5 (e)

Print information available on the last page.

iUniverse rev. date: 01/10/2018

Co- Authors:

Stacy D. Coward
Lucinda Parker "Ms Cindy"

Dedication

This book is dedicated to all those people who are looking for direction in finding their way through the journey of life. Everyone seems to have all the quick fix answers but the truth is it takes work and lots of it. Every day we have to work on being the best person we can be for that day. We have to make a daily decision to live a life that is full of love, kindness and patience toward others. The fact that you are reading this book means that you are on your way. Things bother you that don't affect other people. You have a need to make a change and be the change. You are at critical level most days as you go through your day. It is a challenge for you to act normal, get a job, go home and watch TV like the rest of the world. We write this book to encourage you in the hope that it will help you to write a new story for generations to come. You are a trailblazer. You were born for this level of intensity. You can stand it. You can do it. God has equipped you and created you in a wonderful fashion. God built you for this stuff. Allow God to lead you on your mission and allow Him to give you all the resources, people, energy and supply that you need to accomplish your Great Work! This is your Blueprint to Success!

To God Be All Glory and Honor and may He bless you greatly on your journey towards success!

Introduction of Authors

Ms Cindy

Mrs. Lucinda "Cindy" Parker

"If you tell me where you want to go, I can get you there!" God will use people as a vehicle to help you to understand the "How to's" for success. Miss Cindy is that vehicle. She has a countenance of a queen adorned with grace, elegance, intelligence and beauty. God has equipped her with knowledge, understanding and wisdom for building families, communities and businesses. She is a well sought out business woman, entrepreneur, and financial advisor in a diverse arena of knowledge from hair care to health care. She is a "Dime" to our community, country and world. She has a gentle way of translating information on how business success works. She is polished in wisdom and can deliver a plethora of knowledge to any audience. When Lucinda "Cindy" Parker speaks everybody is listening. She is worth her weight in gold!

One of the most powerful principles that Miss Cindy has taught me during our journey is to stay encouraged as we patiently await God's daily provision and His promises. She has helped me to believe that I am ready! I want to share the foundational pillars I have learned to live: "Know that you are well able to complete your journey and you are equipped to do all that God has assigned to your hands. So smile, love, laugh and give as much as you can during this journey. Embrace the changes and do not be afraid for they are only here to guide our steps. There is nothing that God has not equipped you for. You only think the thoughts you do because it is needed was for your journey. God thinks to us! God has given you every provision that you need at your fingertips to finish your assignment. He has already provided you with all the resources, gifts, people, knowledge and understanding at the conception of your life. "Thoughts become Words that become Things!"

Thoughts- Believing that God has already provided everything you need for this journey and the assignments of your hands.

Words- Using your words to edify yourself as you are waiting and working

Things- Being prepare to receive gifts at this level of responsibility

Stacy D. Coward

My real life began in June 1996 when I turned my life over to Christ and let Him begin to lead and guide me. My life changed when I started understanding how to hear and see what God was doing. My life became purposeful when I started allowing God to direct and order my footsteps for His glory and honor. He allowed me to serve thirteen years in the United States Army National Guard as Army Nurse ranked as Captain, while working as a Psychiatric Registered Nurse for over twenty years. By the grace of God I am also a Licensed Professional Counselor . I currently serve as the senior pastor of local community church and I am pursing my Doctorate in Theology. About ten years ago, God began to speak to my heart to equip His people with everyday basic living skills, educational enhancement, employment readiness and success training. However, all I could do was to give them a big hug. I felt defeated. I was not able to give people a real chance at success by providing them real resources, tangible information and evidence based practices that could change their lives. During the next ten years, God blessed me with a new knowledge to help people become their greatest asset. I remember the day of the paradigm shift in my thinking. I was driving down the street and God said, "Look over there." I saw a small sign on a white door that read Counseling. All I could think was I don't want to listen to any more problems. I just need answers for all of this stuff. I had four children by the time I was twenty three and had experience enough drama to last a lifetime. I had heard enough problems! Little did I know, it would be the foundation for the great work of serving God's people. Some years later, God blessed us to develop programs with lessons that we taught each day that would become framework for The Blue Print for Success.

About Our Programs

We have been empowered to assist in the transformation the community of Portsmouth, Virginia. Our programs as of this date have served thousands of people with educational resources, counseling, social welfare programs, job placement opportunities, life skills training, mentoring programs, youth mentoring programs, fast track educational programs that lead to immediate hire with ninety percentile job placement, housing for veterans and mental health population, mental health counseling for families and individuals, alcohol and substance abuse program and much more. We have been blessed and I am grateful and honored to serve our community.

Question: Did you start your day in prayer?

Prayer for Success

When in doubt read this AGAIN and AGAIN

Father God in Heaven in the name of your son Jesus I thank you for being in charge of all things. You are the author and finisher of all things therefore I command all things great and small to come into alignment with what God is doing. Every heart, every mind, every resource, every person will come to attention and walk with intentions and commitment to this GREAT work. Lord I completely surrender my will to your way. Have your way this day. I call forth every GREAT work for myself. I bind all opposition. I bind jealousy, envy, malice, anger, frustration, slow fullness and inconsistency. I lose love faith, health, tenacity, fortitude, peace, resources and finances over myself and all those who are affected by my life's journey. Thy kingdom come thy will be done this day and forever more. Amen and Amen!

As a final thought to my brothers, my sisters, my fathers, my mothers, be encouraged and keep moving. Today is your opportunity to seize greatness. Seize the day! Work with diligently and accuracy. Fear not and get it right the first time. You can do this!"

To God Be All Glory and Honor and may He bless you greatly on your journey towards success!

Contents

Acknowledgements

We give God all glory and honor and we take no credit for the work and insight of this book. God is the author and finisher of our lives. It is the Spirit of God that leads us, guides us and protects us. That principle of understanding is the glue to your *Blueprint to Success.* Everything we are, everything we will ever be all comes from God. He has been the reason we are able to finish. ***Trust in the Lord with all your heart and lean not to your own understanding. Acknowledge Him in all your ways and He will direct your paths. Proverb 3:5-6.*** Ms Cindy and I are so grateful that God brought us together to finish the race. God has blessed us both with wonderful husbands and outstanding family members that stand beside us and allow us to shine. We have supportive families and friends and we thank God for all the love. God bless you and we love you.

Introduction

To God be ALL glory and HONOR,

This book was developed through a collaborative effort from friends and family. We have successfully created a wonderful tool for practical applications of success principles. We used the life lessons, knowledge, strategies, execution and evaluation to help us to uncover and discover the techniques and tools for success. These strategies will help you to navigate your lives towards health, wealth and prosperity. These biblical based God center life applications will help you to focus on the source for your creation who is God. They help uncover and generate the resources that He has put at your disposal. These tools facilitate a health and wealth philosophy for living. They provide the framework for the resources that are needed to create mental, spiritual, physical and financial health and wealth sustainability practices for generations to come. The lessons in the book tell you how we got over to the other side and stayed. The purpose of the book is resource to teach, reach and realize personal success.

Question: What do I hope accomplish by writing this book?

I want you to believe that you are worthy to have a successful life. I want to be one of the first people to encourage you into your life of success. You can make it! You can do it! You are well worth the battle! You are worth fighting for! I care about your success and I believe in you. Now, you have to believe in yourself! One of the greatest misfortunes I have seen has been people with great potential failing to believe that they were worthy of a better life.

I believe that the power of God has the ability to transform ourselves into anything that we can imagine. If we can recognize that God loves us and He has created us to live an abundant life that is full of every kind of richness. Health, wealth, generosity, love, happiness, humility, joy and peace are all riches. You are worthy to live a life that is abundant in full circle. Most people with great potential only need some word hugs, a pat on the back and a genuine, a "You can do it!" to help them to see their lives in full blossom. The problem is not being able to hold on to the dreams when opposition comes.

This book will help you to establish techniques and create patterns of thinking that will fortify your vision for success. The first instruction I want to give you before reading any further is to commit to doing everything that is written in this book for at least sixty seven days in order to establish success habits. These are research based techniques that will make life changing impact for everyone who does as this book instructs you to do. The second instruction to creating your blue print to success is to go to the mirror, look at yourself and speak these life words:

"I have been created to accomplish the purposes of God therefore He has equipped me with everything I need to become a success. Thank you, God for providing every resource for my success. I believe it is on the way! I AM worthy to receive God's blessings for my life. In return for the blessings that you entrust to me, I will provide a valuable service and work with a servant's heart."

Bought Sense Nuggets: Value yourself .....if you don't no one else will**. Charity**

Question: How to use this book?

This book is formatted to be used as a practical tool for your ongoing growth and development. Read the book several times and refer back to the charts and tools as reference points for helping in your decision making processes. As you are reading this book highlight, circle and complete the exercises.

1. Use the systems to track your progress.
2. Use the book along with a journal to really explore you thoughts, feelings, goals and dreams.
3. Basic Principles are ideas that you should start thinking about to reshape your thinking patterns.
4. Memory verses are noted throughout the book. There will be several scripture references to build your character and ignite your potential. Commit them to memory.
5. The "5 Why's" techniques should be used for every question. Each section poses a question for you to explore your feelings.
6. The "Questions" are there to prompt you to explore your feelings. Answers the questions using the 5 Why's techniques which answer Who What When Where Why.
7. There are mindfulness techniques that will help you to focus on whatever area you need to gain insight in.
8. The accountability practices help you to keep track of where you are and what you are actually trying to accomplish.
9. Defining Moments are located in the beginning of the chapter. Refer to the Defining moment gauge when you are faced with a challenge. This defining moment gauge

prompts you to ask yourself the question: Does the decision line up with our defining moment gauge for success?

10. Use the Defining Moment Scale as a check point for you thinking verses your behavior. Keep a check whether or not the behaviors you are displaying are aligning with the defining moment gauge for success.
11. The best gifts in life, money cannot buy. As the grown up folks say, "Bought sense is the best sense!" Throughout the chapters you will find the Bought Sense Nuggets i.e. the mistakes of others! The most successful people are able to capitalize on the mistakes of others and grow from their mistakes. These are the life lessons that were learned the hard way and they have been passed down from the older generations. These lessons will help you to navigate more proficiently through your success pathway by using the experiences of others.

Chapter One

Understanding the Basics: You are a Creator

Basic Principles:

Your Purpose
Your Power
Your Perception
Your Position

Defining Moments Gauge for accessing your Power in God Memory Verse

Mark 11:23

For verily I say unto you, That whosoever shall say unto this mountain, Be thou removed, and be thou cast into the sea; and shall not doubt in his heart, but shall believe that those things which he saith shall come to pass; he shall have whatsoever he saith.

On a Scale from 1-10 how much do I really believe this Defining Moments Nugget?

0-2 Not at all (This is really hard for me to believe)
3-5 Somewhat (Sometimes I do, Sometimes I don't it just depends)
5-7 Most of the time (I live this way most days)
8-10 All the time (I live this way everyday no matter how I am feeling)

Question: Who am I?

Understanding Your Purpose

Understanding your purpose requires silence so you can hear. The very first thing that you must do is learn how to quiet your mind so that you can hear what is being said and how that will work towards your greatest purpose in your life. Every day we are creating something. Ask yourself, "What miracle can I allow to be created through me today." Every day you are moving closer towards your purpose. In order to understand your purpose you must first understand who you are and whose you are. ***You are a conduit for God to make miracles happen through.*** Open yourself to be used by The Miracle Maker. If you have any obstacles in your life that are stopping you from becoming all that God has created you to be stop right now and command them to simply go away! If there is anything that you need to assist you in becoming who you are simply command them to come! Your purpose allows you to easily call things as though there were because you were created to do that assignment. All of the people, money, resources, information will be at your disposal because it is what you were made to do. Your purpose gives you authority to call certain things into place that only you can call into place because it belonged to you from the beginning of time. It is necessary for you to complete your assignment. There is great purpose in your life and therefore there is no such thing as a coincidence.

Coincidences are never coincidences that are always a necessary part of the journey no matter how insignificant they may seem. Often times people may think to themselves I wonder why this happen. It is actually a clue into the next part of your journey. Most people are not settled enough to read the clues of the universe. God has already provided everything you need from the beginning of time and all you need to do is to get to the place where the resources are waiting for you. God has angels ready and waiting to be dispatched on your behalf to provide, guide, defend and protect you. God has angels disguise everywhere that are assigned to your life to help you on this journey. He has ravens prepared to bring you meat and He has prepared the table for you. Your job is to get started on the journey. If you build it they will come! If you believe it God will provide. It is all a part of your purpose in life!

It is important to maintain awareness that all the great things that you have or will accomplish weren't you. An even bigger idea is that none of the success is for you or even about you. If you think that God is going to bless you for one moment so you can go buy you a big house on the water, retire tomorrow, sit down and watch TV, you have it all twisted. God is not in the blessing business to help you to sit down somewhere to rest or retire. God blesses us so we can do more work. He gives us more resources to provide for more people. Your family will always have enough just by virtue of being with you. You are the cup that is filled and the people drink from your overflow. God fills your cup to a place of overflow for other people. You were created to serve others. Everything that God does through you is for someone else. This is a fundamental principle. It's not about you. You were created to be used. We can never say that we feel used. Nobody is ever using you. You were created to be used by other. That is your purpose!

Question: What does power of the tongue mean in the real world?

Understanding the Power of Your Tongue

<u>**Defining Moment on gauging Desire**</u>
"How bad do you want it?" **John E. McDonalds**

Your mouth has the ability to call everything you need into existence and your faith will allow it to manifest itself. As you speak over yourself with daily affirmations of greatness you will begin to see the manifestation of greatness. The universe is made up of energy vibration that response to the vibrations that are coming from your mouth. If you tap the key of C on a piano the second piano in the room will begin to vibrate on the same key of C. That is how our tongue works. The words that we speak out into the atmosphere connect to the energy that you have spoken. I spend my words for the day on thoughts and ideas that bring me health, wealth, abundance, love, gentleness and kindness. I do not allow my words to be easily spoken. Nor, do I randomly speak about people or things that I do not believe will increase their well being. For example, conversation starting with, "She is crazy. He was stupid, that idiot said." Those are the conversation that I try to quickly end. Those words will always result in negative outcomes for someone. For every one negative word I speak requires two positive words to get ahead. I am careful on how I use my tongue. My words have power therefore I chose them wisely. You are the sum total of everything that has been spoken over you the past ten years. We are living on a ten year delay. The things that you see occurring in your life today are a direct result of what you were exposed to ten years ago. Your life is a direct result of the words that were spoken out of your mouth ten years ago and what you allowed to manifest itself as a result of what you said you would or wouldn't do, could or couldn't do, should or shouldn't do. There are no coincidences you are the accumulation of the words that have been on your lips for the past ten years. Your mouth calls up coincidences and happenstances every day. We are seeing the results of what has been on our tongues daily. As you walk down the street or go about your daily activities things will just happen that you had thought about and spoke about. Have you ever said, "I was just talking about your the other day." As you begin to understand your tongue and how to use it for your benefit you will "happenstance" upon the people, places and resources that you need to accomplish your mission. We must make a conscious effort to assign a watchman on the wall of our tongue. You can't say everything you feel like saying. We must constantly monitor or watch our language to make sure that you are speaking life statements into existence. We must be make sure that even when you do feel doubt it is counteracted by a positive belief system and positive words that contradict your fears.

Exercise to increase your understanding

The tongue literally moves universe.

Try these tongue power exercises

Your words move the universe.

If you speak the words "Speak life" on a feather it will move it. Anything that moves ultimately moves something else whether it is air, water or even an object. Our words create a direction for how we use our energy.

Your words have the power to strengthen you or weaken you.

Have someone to hold their arms up to the side while standing on one foot. Tell them to say all the positive things they can think of while you are pushing down on their arms. You will not be able to push their arms down.

Do the same exercise with them saying every negative thing they can think of and you will be able to push their arms down.

Your words have the ability to produce change

Carefully, put both hands together as though you are about to pray. Make sure you align them from the lines starting at the wrist. Make sure all your lines on your fingers are aligned.

Speak to your left hand. This time say, "Hand grow longer" (Seven times).

What do you see?

Do the same exercise this time say, "Hand go back." (Seven times).

What do you see?

Whether you agree that it was your mouth that created the change or your perception through the power of persuasive thinking.......... the point is........ change occurred after you spoke! If you did this exercise correct.

Question: How do my thoughts affect my life?

Understanding your perceptions

Everything comes from your thoughts. The mind and body experience cannot differentiate between what is a dream and what is reality. That is why if you have someone to talk about something that really made them angry twenty years ago. If you allow them to talk about it long enough their heart rate will increase, they sweat under the arms and they will even get aroused about the conversation. Most people will stop the conversation when they feel themselves getting upset and say, “I don’t want to talk about it.’ The reason is because the mind prompts the body to respond to thoughts that are being played in our heads. The body’s reaction to the stimuli is still the same as though it were happening right at that moment. You are able to experience the feelings at the moment of thought as though it were actually happening. Remember the body will always follow the mind. That is why it is so important to be aware of how powerful your imaginations are and you must bring every negative thought under subjection immediately.

Memory Verse
2 Corinthians 10:5King James Version (KJV)
Casting down imaginations, and every high thing that exalted itself against the knowledge of God, and bringing into captivity every thought to the obedience of Christ;

Question: Who qualified me to be a success?

Understanding your Position in this Earth

You were born to create! ***Genesis 1:28 God blessed them and said to them, Be fruitful and increase in number, fill the earth and subdue it, Rule over the fish in the sea and the birds in the sky and over every living creature that moves on the ground.*** From the beginning of time we were set up to be in charge, to multiple and subdue the earth. That is your position. God has put his stamp of approval on your success. God has determined our position to be above and not below. We are the head and not the tail, the lender and not the borrower. We have been positioned to do great and wondrous miracles. ***John 14:12 Most Assuredly, I say to you, he who believe in Me the works that I do will he also do, and greater works than these will he do because I go to My Father.***

Most people do not have a problem believing that they are able to have success or greatness. The challenge is getting people to understand the correct method for obtaining success or greatness. They often get out of the correct position. The correct position knowing that you have everything that you need to do what God has called you to do! They only need to call things to them. People do not understand their position which involves a position prayer that seeks direction, built up in faith words and having the correct activity. The next time you feel as though you are not making progress, check your position. What does your prayer time, your faith words, your movement and your time spent doing what activities look like. If everything is in line then keep it moving and trust God.

Many people do not understand this concept. They hear the words but they do not believe. Instead of believing God and trusting that He knows what He is doing at the first sign of distress people begin to crumble, run, cuss, fight, get two jobs, get a divorce, file bankruptcy, get a payday loan and everything else that reinforces there is a need to self preserve due to a lack. People position themselves in fear and start working from a position of scarcity. The position that they should be holding on to is that of a warrior that refuses to die even in the face of adversity. The position they should be holding on to should reaffirm they are the head and not the tail. You must learn how to work within God's system to acquire your goods. I want you to know that you do have a ticket to ride all the rides because this ticket has been purchased by the Master of this universe. This ticket allows you to ride all the rides, visit every nation, capture every great idea and harness it until it becomes a reality.

You have the ability to move through the environment and create changes that your mind can dream up. Your imagination allows you to understand your purpose. Whatever things that you imagine are for you. The only reason you thought of it is because it belongs to you. Everyone is not having the same imagination as you are having and that is because it is your destiny to fulfill. You were created for your purpose and there is no one alive that can do what you are assigned to do the way you would do it. God has a way of thinking to us His purpose. He thinks to us! When you have an idea the only reason you have it is because it is a part of your destiny.

Technique for identifying your purpose:

1. List all the things that you would do if money were not an issue.
2. What can you do hands down that no one else can beat you doing?
3. What are your natural talents or abilities?
4. What is it that you can do that was not taught to you?

Technique for identifying the purpose of your children

1. What are your children attracted to?
2. What do your children do with ease?
3. What excites your children?
4. What do they ask to participate in?

Question: What do you want?

Memory Verse
Habakkuk 2:2
And the LORD answered me, and said, Write the vision, and make it plain upon tables, that he may run that readeth it

A name a date and dash in the middle

Your life should not be the sum total of a name, two dates and a dash in the middle. Will you leave a legacy behind for your children's children? ***A good person leaves an inheritance for their children's children, but a sinner's wealth is stored up for the righteous Proverbs 13:22.***

Live your life in such a way that the fruit of your labor will be respected and honored long after you passed. There should be an inheritance that lives five to ten generations past your life time. Your work should give your great grand children an opportunity to succeed. Give everything you have to give so that when you have left this world you will have given everything that was in you. The legacy that you leave should carry on for generations to come.

Here are some self awareness questions

1. How do you want to be remembered?
2. What do want to you leave for your great grandchildren?
3. What are some issues that are important to you?
4. How can you become a catalyst for community change?
5. What will be the difference because you were born?

If you are having difficulty answering these questions take a few minutes to revisit your purpose and make sure it is clear and concise.

A clear vision of your purpose will always include an avenue to pour into other people's lives.

Question: How will my dreams and vision of myself manifest itself in this lifetime?

Dream so big it scares you! Don't be afraid to dream as big as you want to dream. Allow yourself an opportunity to be whoever you would like to become with no limitations on what you can have. Amazingly I have found that many people don't dream big enough. If what you are doing doesn't create some level of concern for how you are going to get it done the dream isn't big enough. It should be so big that it does scare you to think about how you could possibly get it done. The great part about it is that you are equipped to get it done and God is in control of making sure it gets done. You have no reason to be afraid because it's not you making it happen. You are only scared because you begin to see the level of responsibility that is assigned to your life. Responsibility is the scary part! Not the Dream. Dream big enough to say….Whoa….Now that's big!

Question: **Whose dream are you working on?**

Never stop dreaming you are wasting valuable time! Dreaming is the part of you that reaches beyond the here and now. Dreams are limitless and without boundaries. When you dream it allows you to see life in a picture that is appealing to you. Dreaming allows you to create a picture of the reality you would like to see for your life. It allows you to have a vision for your future. It is not until you start working on your dream that we begin to see all the counterattacks against the dream you are trying to bring into a reality.

Time is always moving and many times because people do not have a focus on where they are trying to go they are not able to harness their energies into one clear concise direction. That direction is towards the dream. Valuable time is wasted because you end up spending your time working on projects that are not a part of your dream. People end up giving you a part to participate in their agenda and before you know it the day is gone and you have not worked on your dream. Every day you are working on someone else's dream. It is important to work on your dreams every day. Allow yourself time everyday to reset your thinking and focus on what is important for you. You have twenty four hours to work on your dream. Every day you are losing valuable time if you are not working on your dreams.

There is a power attached to your thinking patterns. If you spend your time thinking (dreaming) about what you want, how you will get it or who you need to get it done, you will find that the situations will start aligning themselves to help you along the journey. The reason is because your dreams have the ability to create a flow of energy towards you that will cause people to poor into your visions. Many people do not have a dream of their own that they recognize. The majority of people are just walking around letting life happen to them. They are taking their cues from others and participating in someone else's vision. That is not a bad thing because I know that parts of my dream cause me often to participate in other people's dreams and goals. I just need to know that the time that I spend participating in the dreams of others will have a direct positive effect in getting me to where I need to be in my life. It is important to be aware of where you should be in order to allow God to show you what He is creating and align your actions with His purposes and then be open to His guidance. In your weakness He is strong! Sometimes the dream will seem so great that it's unfathomable. Every day you must allow yourself to be in a place of dreaming about your end result.

Memory Verses

1 Corinthians 2:9 (KJV)

But as it is written, Eye hath not seen, nor ear heard, neither have entered into the heart of man, the things which God hath prepared for them that love him.

Isaiah 41: 10

Fear Not I am thee and I will uphold thee with the right hand of righteousness

Technique for identifying the details to your purpose-

List all the things that excite you? Why do they excite you?

1. What frustrates you?
2. What do you get angry about?
3. What do you dream about?
4. What people do you most empathize with?
5. What stories affect you the most?
6. What do you want to be when you are considered all grown up?
7. What does a picture of success look like to you?
8. What things do you recognize as you are going about your everyday life?
9. What things do you find yourself speaking up on?

Question: What about all the details?

You may not know everything you should be doing but do something! Many times you will not know how you are going to get to the finish line all you know is where you want to end up. It is not important to know all the details for how you will get there especially when you are first getting started. Don't worry about all the details, just know where you want to go and allow God to get you there however He wants to do it. Getting started is the half the battle. Finishing is the other half. You do not have to know how you will get there. You only need to know where you are going. Create a dream based on what your idea life looks like. Your energy needs a place to be directed towards. That is why vision boards are so important. Allow yourself to have a vision of what you what to do and God through the universal laws of attraction will send it towards you. You only have to stay focused on the end results. Leave the details up to God.

Technique for identifying what you want:

If you had a magic wand that your could wave and make your life whatever you wanted it to be, what would that life look like for you? Make a detailed list of everything you want and write it down in a dream diary or dream journals. These are always a good way to capture these ideas on paper. You don't have to know exactly where you are trying to go just allowing yourself to dream begins the journey. When you begin this exercise allow yourself to dream without limitations. Do not put limitations on how you will receive the blessings just ask God to show you what you are eligible for in this life time. Never use journals and diary to write down angry and negative thoughts and save them because whatever you write down, read and think about i.e. meditate on will expand. Use your writing to expand on positive thoughts, dreams, aspirations and goals. Use your journals to expand on what life you are dreaming up for you and your family.

Three important questions you need to ask yourself

Now that you have identified what makes you happy and what your purpose is you are ready to develop a plan that allows you to provide a service for a certain group of people and receive compensation for quality services. Be as specific as possible use details to clearly see where you are going.

Ask yourself these three questions

1. What SERVICE do I want to give to the world?
2. How will I give QUALITY SERVICES to the people?
3. What would I like in return for the SERVICE that I will provide?

Chapter Two

Understanding the Basics: Getting from where I am to where I would like to be

<u>Basic Principles</u>
Plan the dream
Practice the dream
Push the dream
Pull the dream

Defining Moments to gauge your perseverance level:
Do your best even when you don't feel like it... **Charity**

On a Scale from 1-10 how much do I really believe this Defining Moments Nugget?

0-2 Not at all (This is really hard for me to believe)
3-5 Somewhat (Sometimes I do, Sometimes I don't it just depends)
5-7 Most of the time (I live this way most days)
8-10 All the time (I live this way everyday no matter how I am feeling)

Question: What's the Plan?

Planning the dream

Now that you have clearly annotated what your dream is it is time to think about getting there. One of the greatest challenges that I see most often is inconsistently in people and an inability to complete the goals. People become distracted by circumstances, paralyzed by fear or stagnated by a lack of knowledge. Life happens but you have to trust that God has it all under control and HE will not fail to complete the perfect work in you. People's plans do not work because of distractions, fear and lack of knowledge and these are the results of not allowing God to guide them in the right direction. **A man's heart plans his way, but the LORD directs his steps Proverbs 16:9 .** Many times people try to come up with the steps to the plan. We are not God therefore we are not in charge of how God is going to bless us. We must learn how to allow God to be God and work within His plan for success. He is well aware of the desires of our hearts. He knows what we will do before we ever do it. Therefore He has put provisions in place to ensure the plan is successful. People mess up by not allowing God to lead. They try to make things happen and often those things are contrary to what God is saying or doing. The greatest asset a person can have is self discipline. Self discipline is essential to your success. Listening to God as He speaks through people and situations is a skill that must be developed for true success. Allow yourself to be guided into the direction you should be moving towards. Never try to force a plan. A forced plan is not where we should be investing our time. There are gentle tugs and pushes that move us along our journey. If we listen to the tugs, unction, gut feelings and sometimes ordinary folks that God will send to encourage us and give us counsel we would be easily directed.

Bought Sense Nugget:
Where you are is not where you are obligated to stay**....Charity**

Question: What activities do you participate in everyday?

Practicing the dream

If you want to be a famous book writer then you should be writing stories every day. If you want to be the next Michael Jordan then you should be shooting hoops sixteen hours a day. Most people want all the fame and glory but they refuse to put the time in to become great. They never practice the dream. They invest in the wrong people, experiences and activities. They never spend time practicing their dream. When you don't practice you will never believe that you can have what you say you can have. Practicing your dream will allow you to see yourself growing and learning new skills that make you better suited to receive the benefits of your dreams. Practicing your dreams should allow other people look at you life and see that you love writing, art, basketball or singing. You should be able to look at a person's life and see the dream.

Evaluate your life to see if you are practicing your dream

1. Look at your home/work/play and environment. What you really love?
2. Look at your priorities: bank accounts/ receipts. How do you spend your money?
3. Look at who is influencing your behaviors. Who are you spending your time with?
4. Look at how you get through crisis. Who and what do you turn to in your time of need?

Question: What are some of the things that you do on a daily, weekly, quarterly or yearly basis to push your thinking in the right direction?

Pushing the dream

Every year in October is good time to redefine your goals and to check in with yourself to see if you have accomplished what you set out accomplish. Your dreams need you to reignite them. Pushing your dreams requires you to advocate for those things that are important for your life's journey. At the last quarter of each year you should be pushing the closing ideas for that year and establishing new projects, goals and ideas. It is your job to push your dreams! You are the only person that has the real motivation and enthusiasm for your dreams. Everyone around you will help you in your dream but you are the one that has to do the real work. You are the one that has to do the late night hours. You are the one that has to know the final answer. You are the one that has to know all the details. You are the one that has to know the limitations on the projects, the weakness, and the strengths. You are the one that has to actually take the test. There may be many people that are excited for all that you are doing and motivated to assist you in the project but please remember the key word is they are assisting you in making your dreams come true.

Bought Sense Nugget

When it is all said and done it is your little red wagon and nobody cares if you have to push it, pull it or ride it through the finish line as long as you get finished!

Robbie Rawls

Question: What do you do to get past your discouraging moments so you don't waste time?

Pulling the dream

Take time to love yourself. Invest in yourself. Encouragement is more than words that you speak to yourself when you are feeling down. Encouraging yourself is the activity that you create for the lifestyle that you say you want. Encourage yourself by getting up every day and attempting to live the extraordinary life. Even if you fail to live that life one day get up the next day and start all over. Give yourself permission to start over as often as you need to restart. If you fall off your exercise or weigh loss wagon get back on it as soon as you recognize you have fallen off. Sometimes pulling your dreams requires effort to commit to the dream even if you do not see it happening. Continue to work each day as though you are moving towards the final goal.

There are times when pulling the dream requires you to pull off the extra weights. Before the ship goes down they start throwing over all the extra weight. When you are tired, discouraged and dismay that is a sure sign that you need to starting pulling off everything, every person and every extra activity that is draining your resource of energy and not allowing you to get where you are trying to go. It is okay to reevaluate your life. You may decide that you do not need some of the things that you originally thought you needed. Look at life and do an evaluation every time you have finished a major task. You should also evaluate yourself every quarter and every year.

After each major task, event, or paradigm shift has been completed use this tool to evaluate these three key points:

1. What is going right?
2. What is going wrong?
3. How can you make an improvement in your life?

Without judgment write as many answers as you can.

Do not think about why it was right or wrong for this part of the exercise. You only need to identify what went right or what went wrong.

You should list as many thoughts that you can think of for each area. This is completed best with a group of people however it can be used with one person.

WHERE DO YOU SEE YOURSELF IN YOUR FUTURE?

(List your accomplishments in the boxes below)

When I am______years old, I will have ________accomplished

25 35 45 55 65

	Accomplished	Accomplished	Accomplished	Accomplished
1				
2				
3				
4				

Technique for the developing the plan

Think about where you would like to see yourself at certain times or benchmarks in your life. This is only a rough draft. It does not have to be perfect it is only a projection of what you think you would like to accomplish. As we gain more knowledge and experience we are changed. Those changes help to create new guiding principles for our hopes, dreams and goals. The most important thing about developing a plan is to begin the process by writing. As long as it is in your head it is only an ideal. It does not become a plan until you start scripting the information on paper. It becomes a working plan once you start making the changes based on the new information that you learn.

As you begin this process allow yourself to dream about what the good life looks like to you and what tangible things you would like to have in your picture of a good life. Who are the people you want around you? What does the house look like? What kind of car are you driving? What do your relationships look like?

Give yourself realistic goals that allow you the time to accomplish the goals. Keep it simple and specific. If you want to own twelve houses but your credit score is 500. Then set the goal on fixing your credit to buy your first house. Dream big but start small. Start with the resources that you have at your disposal. Start the plans involving as least amount of people as possible. If at all possible only include yourself on the responsibilities for completing the task. It is always challenging holding people accountable especially if they are not on your payroll. Even then that can still be a challenge. Set your goals based on what you are able to do. Include others in your goals as your resources expand and permit you to tie their commitment to financial compensation.

SMART by George T. Doran

Goal:

<u>Verify that your goal is SMART</u>

Specific: *In five words or less want do you want?*

Measurable: *What does that goal look like when it is complete?*

Achievable: *Identify the resources: time, money and people that you need to reach this goal*

Realistic: *Why do you want this?*

Timely: *When do you want to complete this goal?*

Important Questions

1. What do I need to do to make it happen?
2. What needs to be developed in my life?
3. What actions need to be completed?
4. What are the barriers to my success?
5. Who will be held accountable for getting each assignment completed?
6. When will the assignment be started and completed?
7. What resource do we need?

Time **Money** **Expertise** **Support**

Priority Indicators

How important is this on our priority list?

HIGH MEDIUM LOW

Accountability

Assign at least two indicators to determine if you are on target for completion. The indicators must be ***measurable in numbers***

Example: By June 30th I will have 6 out of 12 items completed on the list

Tracking should be checked by splitting the time allocated into 3 equals check in dates

1. What is our status?
2. How close are we to completing this task?

Status for being completed

1. GREEN On Target = 50% of the goal is met
2. YELLOW Not on Target= less than 50% of goal is met
3. RED Pass Due=less that 25% of goal is met

Categories of Decision Making

1. Emergent- Will cause long term loss of income, relationships and resources within the next 7 days
2. Urgent- Will cause potential losses if not corrected within the next 30 days
3. Need- Could make the circumstances problematic if it is not corrected in the next 90 days
4. Want- Could make the circumstances easier but it is not necessary to the success in 90 days

Covey's Time Management Quadrants-*Stephen Covey 7 Habits of highly effective People*

1. **Urgent and Important**. These are the tasks you have to do or else you will face negative consequences.
2. **Important and Not Urgent** - This is the quadrant where you want to invest most of your time. Tasks in quadrant two are in direct alignment of your goals and things you want to achieve in the long-run
3. **Not important and Urgent- Also called the quadrant of deception, people often confuse important tasks while in fact they are not important.**
4. **Not important and Not Urgent-**Quadrant 4 contains the tasks you want to avoid as much as possible.

Chapter Three

Table Talk

Basic Principles
Think About it
Meet About it
Be About it

Defining Moment Gauge for seeking counsel
"Everyone should not be seated at your table so be careful when sitting at the Queens's table you might lose your head!" Ms Stacy

On a Scale from 1-10 how much do I really believe this Defining Moments Scale?

0-2 Not at all (This is really hard for me to believe)
3-5 Somewhat (Sometimes I do, Sometimes I don't it just depends)
5-7 Most of the time (I live this way most days)
8-10 All the time (I live this way everyday no matter how I am feeling)

Question: Who is listening to your thinking?

Every person needs a think tank of people with one common goal to work together to make sure the assignment gets completed. ***Proverbs 11:14 Where no counsel is, the people fall: but in the multitude of counselors there is safety.*** These people are the groups that know what they are talking about. They are the subject matter experts in the area. They are experienced in getting this particular project completed. Never underestimate a person who has done what you are trying to accomplish based on what they appear to be today. Even if they have failed in what you are trying to do they are still very valuable. You can learn very quickly what they did wrong and how you can prevent your team from making the same mistakes.

It is important to have a complete thinking team. You need someone young and innovated, someone older and experienced and someone that is able to mediate between the two generations. You should have a minimum of three people thinking along with you. Never make decision based on one other person's recommendation. Speak to several experts and make sure you maintain a table of advisors that are multigenerational as well as versed in many different method of accomplishing your goals.

Question: How often do you get counsel to evaluate your progress?

Set aside a time weekly to evaluate your progress. The meetings should be held at the beginning of the week lasting no longer than 45 minutes. There should be a specific agenda to be discussed. Each person should leave the meeting with assignment and should be able to report on the progress of the previously assigned task. Surround yourself around those who can offer you advice as you go. Get the advice from the subject matter experts but also be willing to listen to the new guy on the block as his perspective may be coming from something that you have not thought about. Be careful that you take in the advice from wise people who have come out from where are you currently standing and have a proven track record for success. Every person needs a think tank of people with one common goal to work together to make sure to assignment gets completed.

Question: When do you get started on making things happen?

Setting intentions for your thought process is done the night before. All thinking about how to accomplish your goals should be done the night before. Yes it is "Now, I lay me down to sleep," but I am prepping for tomorrow by asking God to show me the agenda for tomorrow. As I settle down for the night allowing my mind to rest without any particular agenda that I am putting in place I allow God to show me His agenda. He has a plan and He will show it to us in the form of dreams and words that we hear while we are resting. When you go to bed do not set any particulars on how you will allow God to give you the desires of your heart. He already knows exactly what to do. You are only setting intentions on what you would like. You never set intentions on the how to get it done. You must allow God to tell you that part.

When you get up in the morning your mind will guide you into the direction that will move you towards that goal. For example: You will hear a repeated thought, or remember a part of the dream that stands out. As you are doing your morning preparation to start your day the person or thing that you need to make contact with or who it applies to will come into your remembrance. As you learn how to quiet your mind you will be able to hear more quickly and more clearly.

It is important to have a clear direction for what is important for today. Preparation for today starts last night. Each day needs to be assigned to a particular work. Before you go to sleep ask God to give you direction for the plan for tomorrow. Thank him for the guidance he has given you for today and lay down expecting Him to guide your directions for tomorrow. Use sleep mediation practices to allow your mind to settle down. Avoid caffeine's, candy, coffee TV's playing in the background, lights on or other activities that keep your mind stimulated. The goal is to have your mind as quiet as possible before you go to sleep so you can see and hear your direction for tomorrow.

Question: How do I know when not to meet?

Don't waste time in a bunch of none productive meetings. Many people get caught with time wasters of meeting before or after the meetings. Trust the people you meet with and or don't meet at all. After the initial meeting the rest of the meetings should be about follow up. The follow up should be annotated in numbers. Measurable outcomes are the numbers that are produced after all the talk is done. People who talk are just that — all talk. Stop talking and start working. Show me the numbers and I will show you the money i.e. productivity! The Think Tank meetings should be power brains coming together with the best ideas, most resources and most easily deliverable quality services. After these decision makers have come together it is time for the production team.

Person Responsible	Task to be completed	Expected Date of Completion	Potential Barriers to Success	Resources Needed
Stacy				
Cindy				
Diana				
Robert				
Mike				

Chapter Four

Ear Talk

Basic Principles
The right people
The right conversation
The right thoughts
being validated

Defining Moments to gauge if you
have the right person in your ear
If ALL else fails…… Fall Out!"
Robbie Rawls
(Laugh out Loud)

On a Scale from 1-10 how much do I really believe this Defining Moments Scale?

0-2 Not at all (This is really hard for me to believe)
3-5 Somewhat (Sometimes I do, Sometimes I don't it just depends)
5-7 Most of the time (I live this way most days)
8-10 All the time (I live this way everyday no matter how I am feeling)

Question: Who is checking behind you?

Find a mentor that is truly invested in your success. A real mentor will give you assignments, directions, instructions, leadership, guidance and even protection. But the greatest gift I believe they can give you is the phrase, "Let me see."

Let me see means I am holding you accountable for the information I have given you. Let me see means I care that you succeed. Let me see means I want to see that you have done everything I told you too and that you have completed it as I have instructed you to do it. Let me see means I am very proud of you and I can see that the time, money and energy investments I have made in you are worth my time. Let me see means I want to gauge where we started and where we have made it to and what else needs to be completed in you. God is good because many times after He has given us an assignment He will say, "Let me see it". When God says, "Let me see" those are the times when we are placed on the stages of integrity and character check in's. On the "Let Me See You" stage we are placed front and center so that parts unknown to you may be challenged, identified and downright crucified! There is some stuff lying dormant in you that you are not even aware of that God has to get rid of before He can allow you to move to the next level of success. Your true character does not get evaluated until you are in the face of adversity. It is easy to be kind to people, honest in your financial matter and respectful to those you love and appreciate you. However, "Let Me See You" when you are getting cussed out, lied on, cheated on and talked about. That my dear is the true testament of your character development and level of maturity! When you are faced with opposition know that when the flesh is weak the spirit is strong and God is saying, "Let Me see you!" We must always be careful to acknowledge Him and recognize when we are on stage and that our words and actions are being evaluated. The greatest lessons that I try to remind myself about is maintaining humility as God grows me. I really need to be aware of my attitude, my words, my intentions, my behaviors, my emotions, my actions in everyday life. I NEED God to show up on me in everything that I do. I need Him to be in my lifestyle, my appearance, my side bar conversations, the parking lot conversations, the angry conversations, the secret conversations, the thinking conversations. There is a need to be evaluated so you can be consecrated for the Great Work! The promotion cannot come until there has been an evaluation on the work you have previously completed. At the end of the day, I can hear God saying, "Let Me see you!" God is evaluating where we are and how we are using the resources He has given us. God is determining if we are ready to move forward. Remember there is no promotion without a test of faith, character and love.

Bought Sense Nugget:
Do it JUST like I told you. Don't leave out parts of the ingredients and expect success!
Uncle Mike

Question: Who is speaking over your life?

It is okay for you to tell the people who are speaking word curses and death words over your life to get off your set! God is the author of your life story but you are the director. Think of yourself as the person who determines who gets the starring roles in your story. Who will be the people that you surround yourself around to help you become everything that you were called into this world to accomplish? If you have people in your circle that do not honor the very essence of who you are then they should be eliminated. Every person in your ear should speak life into your future existence. If not they need to be kicked out of your script. Don't even give them lines to speak in your script of life. If they try to speak erase their characters from the very pages of your story. Remember this is your life, your story, your world and everybody else is a squirrel for your world. You never have to allow yourself to be subjected to their folly of words that are damaging to you and your foundations for success. Today you are the sum total of every word that has been spoken over your life for the past ten years. We are merely living out what has been spoken over us ten years ago. When you think about where you are today it is a direct result of what you have allowed to be spoken into the atmosphere regarding your existence.

Memory Verse
Proverbs 18:21
Death and life are in the power of the tongue they that love it will eat the fruit thereof."

Recognize when people speak life statement or death statement over your existence. Today is a great day to begin to script your future through your words. Chose your words and use your words to empower your life into a place of greatness, growth and excellence while honoring God through humility and leadership towards His purposes.

Bought Sense Nugget
Some stuff........ you just don't say! **Mama**

Question: Who is influencing the way you live every day?

One of the greatest gifts of life is having an understanding of whose you are in this world and what your assignment is during this lifetime. We all play a role in life and you must determine which role you will play. Every person in your life plays a part in your world they are called your circle of influence. You must be careful who you allow to become a part of your circle of influence. You decide who and what you will allow them to be in your world. We are all given a script and lines to play out. When you look at the people around you and what roles they are playing in your life you make a daily decision of whether or not they will be allowed to act those lines out in your script of life. As an adult, you are the director of all the things that happen through your life. It is important to monitor all the layers of your inner circle. It is important to have Godly counsel around you that you trust their leadership and direction. You will have many ideas but the counsel helps you to become a success and we are able to gleam from the insight of those who have some experience in what you are thinking about doing. Below is a description of all the people that have influence over your life and help to guide your decision making process one way or another.

Vanguard- Your inner most circle has the most influence over of daily life decisions. These are the people you check with on all your daily decisions. They are in your ear more often than anyone else. You call them in the morning before you start your day. You call them to ask questions about decisions that are on you daily encounters. They are your check in systems for your thoughts and they help to keep you out of daily trouble. They help you to make decision about what to get involved in for the day whether it is positive or negative.

8 hours- The people you spend your work hours with. This could be on the jobs, in school or even at home. These are the groups of people you spend your day with once you put on your clothes, send the family off to their day and you start your day. They determine your daily character traits and reinforce your daily behaviors. If they are late to work every day then you will be late to work every day. If they are well groomed then you will be well groomed because it is what everyone else is doing and you become a product of your environment.

Weekly- These are the people who you make an investment in. You generally pay money to be a part of this group. It includes: church, organization, family night or even Friday night party groups. These groups remind you of who you are. These people help to reinforce how you want the world to view you as a person. Everyone stops once a week to engage with this group of people. This is the group that you identify with and it says, "This is who I am!"

2 to 3 times a years- Your reality checkers! You only see this group two to three times a year but they have the most powerful influence on your decisions. They are the people who knew you back in the day when you were getting a free lunch and they can see through all your facades. They look at you and say, "Wow you look great! What have you done? I am REALLY proud of you because you had to work hard and it has paid off! On the other hand they say, "What in the world is going with you? You can fool some of the people some of the time but you can't fool me!" This is the group who tells the truth, the whole truth and nothing but the truth. When they get finished talking to you it will cause you to get up and make a major life move; get a divorce, move out of state or even quit your job. These are people who you check in with 2 to 3 times a year and they help you to gauge, evaluate and adjust fire as needed. They are extremely important because they can give you a true reality check!

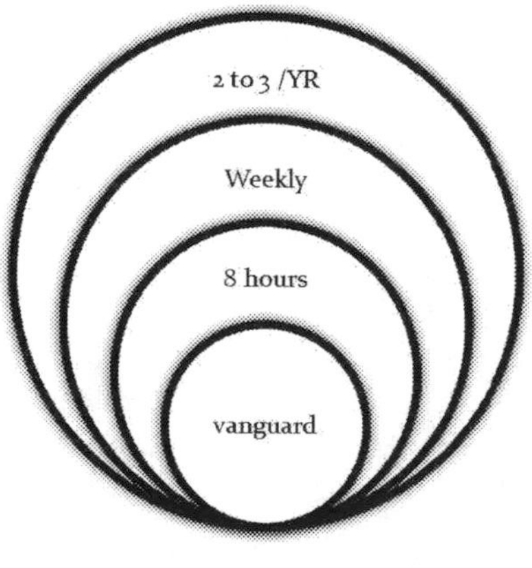

Question: Who told you that you were naked?

Somebody lied to you and made you believe that you were not covered. You are walking around as though you should be ashamed or perhaps you feel as though you are not good enough. Well, the Devil IS a lying wonder! You are beautifully and wonderfully created. God has created you just the way you are and God has covered you. He has your back. He knows everything about you and He knew that you would do exactly what you did. It's okay. Talk to God not man. God is the only approval you will ever need. You don't need the people to validate who you are in Christ. If you ask God to forgive you and truly turn from those ways that are displeasing to God he will forgive you and throw your past into the sea of forgetfulness. Every circumstance in your life that has occurred was supposed to happen. It was written in your deck of cards to play. Some people know how to play the hand of cards they were dealt or people do not. You have nothing to be ashamed of. There was something in this part of the journey that you needed and this was a "must needs to situation". You don't understand the situation but it needed to happen and you will understand it by and by as time goes on.

It is extremely important to have the right thoughts validated make sure that whoever is in your ears is singing the right song in your ear at all times.

I declare and I decree: You are the head and not the tail. You are more than a conqueror. God has given you the power to make wealth. Your children are blessed. You are more than able to accomplish all that God has assigned to your hands. You are healed in your mind, body and spirit. You are at peace. You have more than enough. You have all your needs met and the desires of your heart are coming forward this very moment. You are God's chosen vessel and He has equipped you for this journey. You are Gods handy work and He is invested in you. You shall live and not die. I declare and decree these and all God's blessings over your life today and for all the generations of your family through eternity!

Bought Sense Nuggets

Sounds like a personal problem to me so keep it moving. **Robin**

Now baby, tell me the truth ...... cause I love you we can get through it together. **Mama**

I can't tell NOBODY this one! ...Some stuff you need to take to the grave with you! **Robbie Rawls**

Chapter Five

Ready, Set, Go!

Basic Principles Planning the Plan Working the Plan Finishing the Plan	**<u>Defining Moment gauge for the Rules of Engagement:</u>** My mama says it best, "Get busy living or get busy dying….. But do something! Don't have me waiting on you!" **Robbie Rawls**

On a Scale from 1-10 how much do I really believe this Defining Moments Scale?

0-2 Not at all (This is really hard for me to believe)
3-5 Somewhat (Sometimes I do, Sometimes I don't it just depends)
5-7 Most of the time (I live this way most days)
8-10 All the time (I live this way everyday no matter how I am feeling)

Question: How long will it take me to get there?

Preparation requires movement which in turn equals progress. Movement is required in your thought process. Movement is required in your intention level. What do you intend to have and how have you prepared yourself to receive it? Preparation is a conscious decision to be ready when the prize arrives. You must physically prepare yourself to receive the next level of success. If you want to receive a new wardrobe you must go into your closet and empty out all the old clothing. You must make room for the new clothing and be willing to get rid of the old clothes without the fear that they will not be replaced. The work is in the preparation. The preparation is the part of the cycle that people try to avoid most. The preparation is what makes things easier. Front loading for your success always puts you ahead of everyone else. Much of the current cycle you are currently living in is a result of the amount of preparation you put in during the last ten years.

This is one of the greatest lessons I had to learn in order for success to be birthed from my ideas. Many times we say that we want a home, car, business, spouse or children but we never do the work that it takes to get them. People will not look at their credit and clean it up. They don't go find out about how to open a business in the local area. They won't even go on the date to get the love of their lives. We should ask questions that help to prepare us to be a success in the next level. Here is a tool called the 5 P's Prior, Planning, Prevents, Poor, Performance. I remind myself of these 5 P's every time I think I have done enough. I ask myself questions that make me think about what I need to do in order to be prepared for my future plans. Who is already doing the business correctly? What do I need to do to clean my credit? Do these clothes look like a person who is prepared to be in a relationship? You must be willing to prepare yourself to receive the blessing. What have you done in preparation to receive the next level blessing? Have you educated yourself to be able to understand the level of responsibility that you will be accountable for? Have you purchased a new outfit, combed your hair, and checked your teeth for food? As funny as these questions may seem they are real questions that we have to get honest about and answer without judgment or presumptions. This has to be done before we can get honest with anyone else. We must be willing to do the work of preparation!

Question: Which one would you rather have magic beans or magic teams?

You need to choose early in the game which one you prefer to have in your back pocket. Will it be Magic Beans or Magic Teams? People holding magic beans are the people who come to your table with great stories of magic beans, giants and golden eggs but you never see the results the magic beans produce in your yard. They are useless at your table. They are the people with all the talk about what they can do or what they have done without any tangible evidence that they have produced what they said they can produce. It is imperative that they are immediately dismissed from subsequent meetings. They are time waster and non producers sucking life from your projects because they do not give their energies toward the project they are only there to draw information and energy from the projects. They steal not only your time, money, energy and efforts but they stop the projects from moving forward because they are the Judas' sitting at the table breaking bread with you and team with a heart that is not genuinely invested in the overall health and wealth of the project or team. You are being sold out every time they sit to the table because they are only taking information to improve their quality of life.

On the other hand you have the people that make things happen on shoestring budgets and never complain. These people work as though they own the company and provide service with a heart of compassion that you cannot buy. They are the Magic Teams i.e. production team. Every person needs a production team. They are the people who are in charge of getting us where we need to go. Whether that is completing a project for a class assignment or renovating a twenty thousand square foot building. The production team's job is to demonstrate that they can get the job done. You can never pay them enough for the work that they do. They are your greatest assets to your company, your team and your family because the work they do is priceless and almost magical. The production teams gets together and discussed any deficits, problem areas or potential crisis. They understand how your numbers work. They evaluate and make corrections as needed to improve and maintain the numbers. Production meetings should always be numbers driven. Stop talking and show me what you are doing in the numbers. Each team member at the table should be responsible for a set of numbers that show productivity. Paperwork should be submitted at each meeting. At the adjournment of the meetings if each person is not walking out of the door with a piece of paper in their hand to help them do the next part of the assignment the meeting was a waste of time. Each meeting should have a new document submitted for review from the previous session.

Question: When should I get started?

You have these 24 hours and that is all that you have because yesterday is gone and tomorrow is not promised. So start immediately! It is always the right time for self improvement you never have to ask is this the right time to for me to do better. If you are not supposed to be working on the project you will not have the resources to complete the task. The resources will always be present when you are on target. Everything, every person, every mentor, every "coincidence" as some people like to call them will just appear when you need it. You will have a thought of what you wish you had. Then all of sudden, whatever it is that you had a need for will present itself to you. This is called synchronicity; thoughts becoming things. Today is the only day you have work today's plan. Tomorrow a new idea will be presented to you. Work in today's dream today. Tomorrow you get a new one!

Chain of Progress

Day 1 - Make a decision whether or not information is valuable to you

Move forward

Day 3 - Make the adjustment to incorporate the changes

Move forward

Move forward to 60 day plan reinforce
Successful patterns

Day 7 – Using of the practices on a daily basis

Address any issues BARRIERS TO YOUR SUCCESS

a. What is the reason you are using to say "I cannot do this because….
b. What is needed for you to have success in your Plan A?
c. Have you created your B, C and D plan?
d. What support systems are missing that create feeling of doubt, fear and anxiety?

Barriers Identified corrected

Day 30 – Evaluate yourself for measurable change as a result of using this method

1. How much has changed since you started?
2. Are you on target for meeting your measurable outcomes?
3. Identify the areas that have created obstacles for you obtaining positive outcomes
4. Continue to reinforce the positive behaviors that are facilitating positive outcomes
5. How much further do you have to go to complete this assignment?

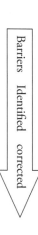

Day 60 - You are completely in the process and you understand how the mechanism works

1. What the requirements are for you to continue?
2. What are some of the barriers to your future success?
3. You are able to read the environment to adjust fire as needed to avoid poor outcomes.

Day 90 - You understand the systems that are needed to maintain sustainability of the new habits and practices

1. Make daily reaffirmations of your commitment to the change.
2. Reinforce your belief patterns by listening to ideas that support you new views.
3. Increase your value by taking courses, classes, certification in the new areas you are developing.
4. Seek out a preceptor or mentor to help you to understand the new and challenging feelings.

Question: What is the problem with not finishing a project?

You are a great started and you have started one hundred projects. The problem is you never finish anything. Ouch! If the shoe fits put it on Cinderella. Your chariot of success awaits you but first we have to deal with this issue. When you begin a project you are planting seeds. Failure to finish projects never allows you to see the fruit of your labor. The seeds never have an opportunity to produce a fruit because you do not allow them to grow out of the ground and develop with strength to bear up or hold up a fruit. Many times people have not even allowed the seeds of their projects to be nurtured and watered before moving onto the next unfinished project.

If you don't get accepted into a program because your scores were too low as a result of not studying you failed the test. You didn't finish. If you are having communication problems with your spouse you won't read a book to help you to become a better communicator. You didn't finish! If you lose your clients to someone who outbids because they can do it for cheaper so you throw in the towel and call it quits. You didn't put in a rebid. You didn't rethink your process. You didn't finish. If you are just breaking even for the first year you say it is not worth it. It is okay that you cannot see a profit in the first year it takes about five years. You were not patient with the process. You didn't finish. If you get rejected by the credentialing agency three times you say, "Three strikes is out!" So now you have a building that you have put your total life saving in with no clients. You didn't finish. You blame it on the devil and say the Lord must not be in it. FOOLISHNESS! I say foolishness. These are all examples of distractions and barriers to your success. I have met people that have started many projects but never finish any of them. They have all these excuses as to why they could not complete the project. I was sick. I lost my job. My dog died. My mama needed some money. You name it there is an excuse.

This is an issue that can drain the very essence of your life from you because you have all these great ideas that never amount to anything. It drains on your life's time. It contaminates your bird eye view on how you perceive your ability to accomplish task. It destroys your faith when you never see anything amount from your hard work. You spend hours preparing, talking, thinking, troubleshooting and even implementing the beginning of the project but as soon as you see a rough spot you abort the mission. This is a problem. Finish it! Even if it comes out with three legs and one eye short finish what you started and tweak it as you go. You can always cut one leg off and buy you an eye to stick up there! The goal is to finish it the polishing will come later.

Question: How do I finish assignments?

When you come to a place where you do not allow excuses to become your reason for not succeeding that is when you will finish the assignment. When you decide to complete the task no matter what happens that's when you will finish the race? When you decide that you will not go any further until this part of the journey is complete that is when you will be eligible for the next level of success?

Question: How do I get past my unbelief that I can finish the task?

Memory Verse

Mark 9:24 *Immediately the boy's father exclaimed, I do believe; help me overcome my unbelief!"*

It is your self- talk that will get you over the humps of discouragement. I always remind myself of this Defining Moment gauge of tenacity "If you believed that the project was good enough to start then it is good enough to finish!" See it all the way through! You have already invested your time into a project and if you do not complete the task you have wasted valuable time that could have produced fruit if you would have allowed it the time, space and energy to grow and develop into its full potential. If you would have let it finish.

There is a certain amount of discipline required to finish projects, goals, assignments or maintain commitments. There is a certain amount of self discipline that each person must bring to the table when doing anything. There has to be a benefit to what something is going to cost you. When I am faced with the challenge of having to push myself I begin to run my list of cost verses benefits to completing the task. There should not be a project that you have entered into without prayer, meditation and guidance. Therefore you should only be working on assignment that God has given you. Then you can go into the assignment with the correct attitude of perseverance which says, "This is my assignment and I am not backing up off of it until it is completed."

You must also have the discipline not to get distracted while you are working on a project this requires daily evaluation of any emotional, physical, financial, and spiritual barriers that were used as the excuse to take a break from the project. Many times there are many reasons to give up. People will talk you right out of your blessing. They will get on your nerves, pride steps in, people start pointing fingers and making unwarranted suggestions. Please be aware it is important to have the discipline of completing the assignment that was assigned to your hands. Do not let the people become a distraction for you. Do not let them move you off your assignment because you became offended by something they said or you started buying into their belief system that does not support where God is taking you. Finishing requires the self discipline to command yourself to keep it moving. You must discipline yourself to default to self encouragement even in the midnight hours. You must discipline yourself not look at today but you will continue on this journey to see what is on the other side. You must have the self discipline to tell yourself that you are not moving on to the next project until this one is complete. No matter how bored, frustrated or worn out on this project you become finish the project.

The next time you start a project ask yourself the following questions,

1. Did I finish the last assignment?
2. What caused you to change your route for completing the project?
3. What cause you shelf the project and move on to the next project?

These all happen because something in you said, "I have had enough of this and I am ready to move on to the next new thing." This can only be controlled through self awareness, a desire to complete the task by finding your "why" and the self discipline to take an honest self evaluation and implement a reasonable plan of action.

Question: How do I use my time the most effectively?

Every morning you should start your day with learning something new. All the new information that you intentionally put in should be done at the start of your day to give you the time to use the information throughout the day. Your brain is fully charged at your early waking hours. That means that you are as smart as you will be right before you are fully awakened. It is that window when you realized that you are no longer sleep and you become aware of the thoughts, sounds and environment around you. The earlier you can catch that moment the more you will be able to download valuable information in that your brain will be able to process more effectively.

Do all of the assignments that require the most thinking power by ten o'clock in the morning. Your brain loses firing power and energy the longer you are awake. You are at your peek smartest when you first wake up and you slowly get "dumber" as the day progresses. Complete all thinking task as early as possible this includes everything that requires a phone call because it allows people to call you back or you to have all questions answered that will stop your progress. If I do not make the phone calls first thing in the morning then it is the last thing that I do so I will have the answer first thing in the morning.

Have a plan on how you will to finish your daily assignment. This should be completed the night before or least before your feet hit the floor the next morning. The details of your plan start in your wakening hours of the early morning prayers and meditation period. The day ends when you have given everything you had in you for that day. You should go to bed empty every night. That means you can barely lift your foot off the floor, raise your arms or keep your eyelids open. When you are at this place then you are finished! The day does not finish at five o'clock. The day finishes when you have poured your very essence out into the world through a project or assignment God has placed in your hands for that day.

Before you lay down at night make sure that everything that you needed to complete in that 24 hour period is completed. The wonderful part about this is that God NEVER gives you assignments that cannot be finished in the day. Even if you have a project that your are working on that will require a year to complete it every day you will have one assignment to complete that will move you closer toward finishing the project. The work for the day is just that the work for the day. All of your tasks should be guiding you towards one direction. All the energy that you spend that day should have a direct impact of the completion of the project. There is no need to rush to get your assignment completed for the day. Just finish each assignment every day.

You have never read any scripture where Jesus ran over here or ran over there. God's yoke is easy. You know you are doing too much when you find yourself moving around being busy but not accomplishing anything. Too much movement is equivalent to no real work being completed. Real work is tangible. You can touch it when it is complete. A lot of movement equals a little work. You must be still to work. People who move around too much are doing activities but at the end of the day you cannot see the results of day worth of work. All jobs that require movement should be done after you have done your thinking work. The jobs that require movement that do not require as intense level of thinking should be done on your autopilot time. Your autopilot times are those routines that you do not have to think about.

Here are examples of autopilot times some of them can be used to do other work while other activities will only allow you to think about what you need to do:

Use this time to use your mind	**Use this time to use your hands**
Washing dishes, taking out the trash, making the bed, taking a shower, straightening your office, Organizing your files, Any sitting time that requires you to wait for someone else,	Walking the halls to make rounds Listen to the people you are servicing and take notes on what is important to them. If you listen most of the information is transferrable to your big picture
Organizing paperwork as long as it does not require your attention for the information on the paperwork	While you are waiting for customers and you have to be in one place carry a pocket sized notebook
Driving to work, exercising, bathing, washing and combing your hair, painting your nails	"Quiet" time at work or home when all the work is caught up and everyone is chit-chatting
Doing laundry, organizing your drawers, cleaning your closets	Any time you are sitting you should have paper and pencil

Cleaning the house, cleaning the car, mowing the yard, planting flowers, sitting outside, walking around the block, looking at the animals in nature, watching the rain fall	If you are "listening" to something you are not interested in but are required to be there. These have been some of my best journaling moments!
Painting a room, cleaning the garage	If you are in the passenger seat you should be writing out your future!

You can use it as waiting times moment to think about new information. This will help you to rebuild or renew what has been taken out during your thinking time.

Technique for finishing Task

1. Always work from a TO DO LIST with a box you can check off.
2. Get a binder for your TO DO LIST.
3. Keep all your task, notes and ideas in a notebook.
4. Use the notebook to follow up on things need to be completed.
5. Each day start with one question: **What is important TODAY?**

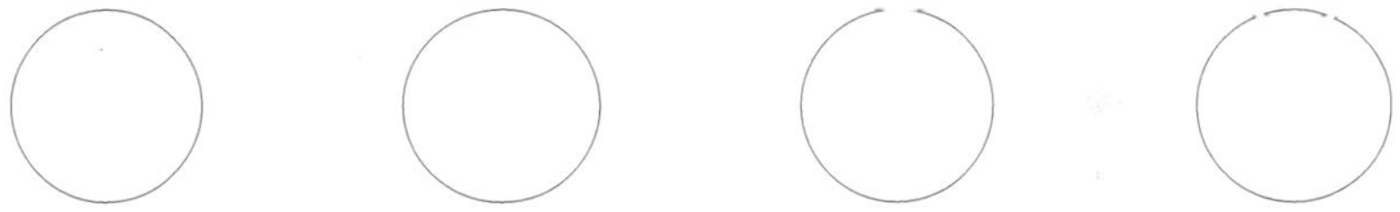

StepOne **Step Two** **Step Three** **Finish**

What steps do you need to take to complete the task for TODAY?

TO DO LIST________ Person Assigned_________ Date________

Done	**Task – Have the building prepared for inspection Next Monday**	**Barrier to completion today**
	Create a spreadsheet with all the names of my clients to include address and phone number	Don't have all the phone numbers and addresses
*	Call the Permits Office to schedule visit	
	Call to pick up the reports by 4pm	Not finished will be finished tomorrow

*	Turn in the Lease by 5pm	
	Call the light company to set up services	Don't have the deposit
	Complete all applications	Left a message to email me the applications today
*	Schedule Dental Visit for Monday or Friday 2 to 4pm	

Make sure that you have created measurable outcomes to include time and date limits. This gives you deadlines and boundaries for completion of task.

Chapter Six

Stumbling Blocks of Success

Basics Principles Obstacles Observations On Time	**Defining Moment for gauging your Strength** *"Lord, you don't ever have to give me anything else if you open up the door for me I will go in and get it myself."* **Robbie Rawls**

On a Scale from 1-10 how much do I really believe this Defining Moments Scale?

0-2 Not at all (This is really hard for me to believe)
3-5 Somewhat (Sometimes I do, Sometimes I don't it just depends)
5-7 Most of the time (I live this way most days)
8-10 All the time (I live this way everyday no matter how I am feeling)

Question: What are your stumbling blocks?

Every day you must wake up and decide you are going to be a better person than you were yesterday and that includes doing whatever it takes to get past your stumbling blocks or obstacles. Stumbling blocks come in all forms, shapes and sizes to include fear, pride, envy, jealousy, slothfulness, undisciplined behaviors and many more. I have heard people say I would have done this but I have so many obstacles in my way. I do not have the support I need. I need more money. I do not have an education. I don't have a babysitter. My credit is bad. Well, fix it! Start today working on something that will fix your problems. I agree that life circumstances will create barriers to your success. Some of them are your fault and some of them are not nevertheless they manifest themselves as lack of finances, lack of social supports, or even a lack of knowledge. Then there are obstacles that you must get past in order to succeed they include: bad relationships, poor credit and poor decisions that have cause you to be worse off than you would have been if you would have corrected the problem sooner. The first task is to recognize that you are the only one that can change your life. No matter how bad anyone else wants your life to be different. You have to want it worse than they do. Secondly, you must correct your self-talk and know that you are the only one who can stop you from getting to your destination. The third task to do is to identify your obstacles. Assessing your situation is very important. Stop for a moment a really take a look at what is causing the problem. What is stopping me from completing this project? Where did they come from? Is this my problem? Is this something I can correct by myself or do I need a support system to correct this? How can I permanently alleviate this problem?

Bought Sense Nugget

Observation is 99% of fixing the problem **...Ashley**

Then put solutions in place that you believe will help to facilitate the easiest route toward accomplishing your goals and circumnavigate those obstacles. Make sure that when you identify your obstacles that you create a plan to fix the problem. This is your A plan. This is the best case scenario plan. This is where many people mess up. They get comfortable and stop pre – planning to make sure the plan works. They reach the first person who says they will help and they say, "Great! Thank you for your help I am not going to call anyone else I am going to depend on you I will see you on Tuesday. Of course Tuesday never gets here and your plan is at a halt. Don't trust anyone to help you fulfill your dreams. Never leave your plans in the hands of someone else. Remember most people are scurrying around with their own agendas and only assist you if it benefits them in some way which could be emotionally, physically, financially or spiritually.

Don't get comfortable with another person income, resources, licenses or building. Remember to get your own especially if this is a major barrier or obstacle to your success. You need to have a B, C and D plan that you have personally verified will work. Check the reliability and validity of each plan by actually making the phone calls to the people as if there were a need for the service or help.

Question: How does this look in real life scenarios?

An example would be to have four back up babysitters. Create two lists: Emergency on call babysitter and Routine back up baby sitter. Call each person to see if they are available today on short notice because you were called into work. If they cannot help you today it is okay remember it is only a drill, find out how much notice they would need to help you in a crisis. You will be able to identify those who are talkers from those who are real supporters. This is important to know before the crisis hits because when you are in the heat of the moment you must have a plan that works without fail. You must make sure your shoes are tied so you cannot trip at the last minute during the race. We were reorganizing my room and it was in a mess and I said to my daughter I don't know where to start she looked around the room and she said let's start with the shoes in the center of the floor they will make us fall. I said to her that's a good one Amarisee. Let's move all the stumbling blocks. What is in your way that would stop you from accomplishing your goals?

Without judgment, list as many answers to the following questions

1. What's going right in my life?
2. What is going wrong in my life?
3. What people or situations are stopping me from reaching my goals?
4. How do I make it better?
5. Who or what do I need to create a positive outcome?
6. How can I get what I need?

Make sure that you set up time lines to benchmark your progression. Remember never be in a rush to finish any projects even if you feel as though you should be further than you are in your life. You are on time! Wherever you are right now is exactly where you supposed to be. You are not late everything that you have learned over the course of time been a part of your journey. It has allowed you to become processed. You needed to experience all these things so you could handle the responsibilities at this a level. The reason why you could not move past a particular place was because you were not ready for the responsibility of the next level of authority. Be patient with other people because they are not on our success timelines so what you think they should have gained from the experience is not necessarily what they will learn from the experience.

Question: Have you bought into your own dream?

You want to get a promotion, apply for a new job, buy a house, start a business, lose weight, go back to school, get married or even start a family. You must first be willing to invest everything you have into the dream. Even if all you have is your last ten dollars invest that into your dream. Many times people want other people to invest in their hopes and dreams but yet they are not willing to use or lose their own money on the project. The first question I ask a person when I am asked to invest in the dream is, "Why haven't you done this yourself? Usually the answer is I didn't have the money or my credit was too bad to get it. My next question is what you have done to fix your credit or get the money prior to this conversation. People generally will accidently disclose that they do have some capital or income but they are not willing to risk it for the idea. Without further ado the conversation generally ends fairly quickly. If you won't buy it then why should I?

The first thing that many people do when it comes to making decisions is automatically assume that they are not eligible to get it. There are all kinds of excuses from bad credit, lack of money, lack of time, lack of support, lack of knowledge and even a lack of willingness to put in the time and energy to commit to their own dreams. If you won't buy into your own dream then why should anyone else. The first step is to think about what it will take for you to get what you want? Then find the motivation, "the why" that will inspire you to want to meet that goal. People always want to jump on the band wagon when the music is playing but what about when the band goes home? You still need to keep the party going and the only way you can do that is through your personal desire to succeed. Your personal desire is your reason. It is the reason why you fight for your dreams. It is the reason why you refuse to die. It is the reason why you get up in the morning and desire to breathe. Believe me for true success to be grounded and rooted in you it has to come from a place deeper than paying a light bill and eating some groceries. Surround yourself with your reasons, remind yourself by using prayer, bible studies, bible scriptures, support groups, community partners, seminars, workshop, educational plans, magazines, books, pictures, words, people and even music to reinforce the direction of your dream. You must be the first person to buy into your dreams. Every day you must make a purchase towards buying into your dreams. You must pay your way! There is nothing that amounts to anything that is free! You must pay some level of cost for your dreams. The cost can come in many forms to include: your time, money, effort, resources, sleep, silence, hands to the plow, volunteer efforts, prayer time, studying the craft, signing up for classes, attending workshops, seminars, obtaining certificates, maintaining the right attitude, meekness in times of adversity, humility when you have a need, working when others are sleeping and so many other forms of cost. You must pay with something! Your dream must cost you something! Then you must campaign daily for your dreams. You have to create the parade to keep your dream alive. You must work on your dreams every day. If you buy into your dreams then other people will buy into your dreams. Remember, you buy it first then come ask me to buy it.

Question: Are you authentic in your intentions?

Before you come to the table to request any help from anyone, get real with yourself first. Your words and your actions should match. Your walk and your talk; they don't match. When you are sincere in your intentions there is no need for checking the facts for reliability. When people are not authentic in their intentions you are able to see through it quickly by seeing what doesn't match. Your words betray you. The language and your "lifestyle" don't match. Your perception on reality is wrong. You are trying to build wealth but you are always backwards hustling by spending your money on all the wrong things and borrowing money to pay your bills. The house you are living in is too big for amount of salary you are bringing home. What are you trying to prove? You are living in the projects driving a BMW and collecting food stamps. What is that about? It doesn't match. It doesn't make sense.

The flip side is deception for example you use words that only someone who has been exposed certain information would used but your are dressed like a common person because you are trying to down play your intelligence to a group of people that your are probably trying to gather information from on the down low. Guess what? We can see you because it doesn't match. Just tell the truth! If you ain't got it. You ain't got it. If you need information then just say you need information.

Question: Has God ever failed you when you trusted Him?

Fear Stops Faith! When you have flashes of fear always remember. "***God has not given us a spirit of fear but power love and sound mind.***" *(II Timothy 1:7)* Unction should never produce fear but awareness. I remember during my early military training my platoon was on top of a tall structure. The drill sergeants were teaching us to repel down the side of a building. It was my turn and the drill sergeant gave the instruction, "I want you to go off the side of the building with this rope tied around your waste." As he was giving me the instructions he pulled on the rope a couple of times ensuring that it was secure. No sooner than he finished talking I took off running as fast I my legs could carry me and dived off the side of the structure. My feet touched the building twice and I was on the ground. I remember looking forty feet up in the air and the Drill Sergeant was lying on his stomach at the top of the building yelling down at me, "Got @#$% soldier! You are one the most diehard soldiers out here! Why did you do that? Still in the rope harness, I quickly yell back, "You told me to Drill Sergeant! I don't have a reason not to trust you Drill Sergeant! Fear is a counterattack on your faith. Imagine if in the middle of me jumping off this structure I slowed down and second guess myself in the middle of the dive that could have gone very bad. Faith drives your energies. Faith is the gas that we need to move from one situation to another, one goal to the next, one accomplishment to the next. Fear puts a halt on your movement. It paralyzes you! Then when it is time to make a decision your decisions come from the wrong place. Every time you allow your decisions to be made based on a spirit of fear you automatically default into a function in error. Nothing good can be birthed from a place of fear. Fear causes pain, distrust, anger, frustration and hurt. Fear causes us to make decision from a place of protection. Fear stifles our ability to be teachable, transparent, giving or even receive from others. Fear is a deadly virus and it can instantly cause you to discard your mission, dreams and purpose. Once fear is identified you must immediately cast down imaginations that create fear. Fear is crippling and can be devastating because it stops your from dreaming and believing in what you do not see. You must first believe it before it will manifest itself. Whatever you are believing God for, you must keep on believing Him for in spite of what you may see with your natural eyes. You must trust that God is working on the plan and believe in His purpose. You must know that God is working through you to fulfill His purpose in you. **Romans 8:28And we know that all things work together for good to them that love God, to them who are the called according to his purpose**.

Question: How do I get from doubt to deliverance?

You have read that you should dream so big that it scares you. Okay, then what? Once you have learned how to dream the next step is to make it a reality. Most of the time we are so far away from the dreams that the mere thought of achieving the dream can become overwhelming. Most of the pitfalls to your success will come from within. These come from mind battles that play out into self sabotaging practice. A person who has not experience successes can sometimes become frighten by prospect of actually succeeding. It is frightening because they have never seen this side of the story before and they are not used to living a drama free life. Looking at life from another bird's eye view can be a scary encounter. Especially looking around the sea of opportunities and realizing that there is another side that you have never seen before. Once you can visualize that other people are actually living on the other side of the mountain. Sometimes people face these mind battle challenges because they don't feel worthy to live on the other side. The other is side is clean, orderly, prosperous and there is an obvious level of commitment to stay on this side. Sometimes that level of commitment can cause people to want to hit the panic button and go back to their comfort zone. If you find yourself sabotaging your growth go back to the basics. Why was I created? What is my purpose? Remind yourself that you are merely walking in your purpose and this is a part of that journey. Walking in your purpose will always produce provision. Instead of reminding yourself of all the reasons why you should not be in the promise land, remind yourself that the people are waiting for you to get in place and this is a mission that only you can fulfill. The whole world is waiting on you!

There are thought stopping techniques that can be used as well as thought pushing ideas. ***One of the techniques that can be used to combat doubt is a thought pushing technique***

In the morning as you are preparing to start your day use motivational speaker audio tools to reinforce your free thought into the correct thinking patterns. These are the thoughts you have during your autopilot activities. The thoughts of fear and doubt will be substituted with the information you are taking in through the motivational speaker audio tools because your brain will only be able to process the information that is new and it needs to filter and categorize the new information. Use as many different motivational speaker audio tools that you need to in order to keep your brain actively listening to the audio tapes. As you are listening to the motivational speakers it will place your mindset in a place of deliverance verses playing out the doubt scenarios.

Other Thought Reinforcement Techniques include affirmations and visual meditations

> *Memory Verse*
> God has not given us a spirit of fear but of power, love and sound mind. (II Tim 1: 7).

Therefore we should always walk circumspective when it comes to moving in faith and God promises.

When you feel yourself going into doubt mode you can easily transition to deliverance with these three steps:

1. Remind yourself, "Hasn't He proved Himself over and over again each day with a brand new mercy."
2. Say to yourself," What has God already done?"
3. Reassure yourself knowing that "The fact that you are reading this book means that He has been good enough to lead, guide and direct you."

He keeps on blessing you! In spite of it all God is good and His mercy is everlasting. God has good intentions for my life and He will never fail me. I just need to trust Him. When I think of His goodness and what he's done for me my soul (which is the place where my mind i.e. emotions) says yes Lord! Command your flesh to trust God. He has promise us so much and we only have to receive His great gifts.

Here is a technique you can use to improve any area of your life but we will use something fun for this exercise!

See it, Hear it, Feel It, Taste it, Smell it

Here are some examples on building relationship:

1. **See** yourself kissing, hugging, communicating in a loving manner, laughing.
2. **Hear** what the sound of the kiss, the tone of a loving manner of communication, the heartiness of the laughter.
3. **Feel** the touch of the lips when you kiss, the embrace of the hug, the gentle touch in a loving manner of communication, the feeling in your heart when you hear hearty laughter.
4. **Taste-** the kiss of the lips
5. **Smell-** the fragrance of the body including the natural body scent. A smell that you can only smell if you are in close proximity.

As you begin to play out these scenarios in your mind you will become exactly what it is that you would like to see in the other person. ***"Be the change you want to see in the world" Ghandi***

What inadvertently happens is as your behavior changes, the other person will respond to your behaviors thus giving you the mirror of what you are giving to them.

Also remember not to penalize people for not meeting your expectation. Too many times we get upset with people that we have put in position that they are unable to fulfill. They were never qualified to be in the position that you gave them and now that they are failing miserably at the assignment, job, role you want to penalize them.

Restorative Prayer

Lord I repent for being angry with this person for failing to be someone that I wanted them to be in my life. It wasn't fair to them and it wasn't fair to me. Help me to move quickly past this place and get back to the business of doing the work of creating. In Jesus Name Amen!

Question: How do I keep it moving after I have messed up?

Say this, "I forgive me." Now let's move on. Even though some days I feel like Popeye and I want to kick my own self in the behind for doing something stupid! I knew better, I had already experience it before and yet I still fall in the hole in the ground. I lost time from having to climb out the hole again. I have learned that one of the fastest ways to come out of the hole is to forgive myself first and allow myself to learn from the mistakes. No judgment, just forgiveness. I forgive me!

Bought Sense Nugget

Stand right there! Don't move! This is going to be a Kodak moment! **Auntie Diana**

These are the times when you do something stupid and you NEED to remember not to do it again!

Just repeat this bought sense nugget as you are coming out!

Say this," I forgive you." Forgiveness is all about you. Forgiveness is never about the other person. Who do you need to forgive? Go buy a card and write these words, "Thank you and Its okay. Everything is all good!" Neutralize the power of the enemy by genuinely forgiving people even if you think you have not offended them. We have to learn how to give up our right to be right so we can move on to the next thing and be blessed. God is love and because of that HE can't sit in all the foolishness that anger, hatred, malice and frustration breed. A non-forgiving heart is always a problem for the person who got hurt. It is a personal problem that you must allow yourself to deal with and release it back into the atmosphere so that it doesn't trap you and keep you from growing. You have to forgive to release yourself from the chains of bondage that come with pain, hatred, anger and frustration. A non forgiving heart stops your ability to create at your full potential.

<u>Using prayer and meditation to give you daily direction</u>

Use prayer and meditation everyday in order to accomplish the skill of quieting your mind. Prayers of gratitude are always a good choice or you may choose.

Memory Verse

The Lord's Prayer
Mathew 6:9-13
Our Father which art in heaven
Hallowed be thy name.
Thy kingdom come.
Thy will be done in earth,
as it is in heaven.
Give us this day our daily bread.
And forgive us our trespasses,
as we forgive those
who trespass against us.
And lead us not into temptation,
but deliver us from evil:
For thine is the kingdom,
and the power, and the glory,
forever and ever.
Amen.

Technique to quiet your mind

After you have prayed, be quiet by using deep breathing techniques in a quiet area with no distractions where you cannot be disturbed. Go to an area where you can allow yourself to lie down in a relaxed position or sit quietly. Focus on your breathing, breath in through your nose out through your mouth while fully expanding your lungs and emptying your lungs four to five times. During the deep breathing exercise hold your breath for four second and slowly exhale through your mouth. During this time distractive thought may come in and out. The stories that you have on your mind will try to play themselves out. Do not allow them to play. Press the stop button. You are able to stop the stories by seeing the thoughts and as your thoughts come in allow them to drift away. Don't hold the thoughts. Don't expand on the thoughts just allow them to leave as quickly as they come in. After a few minutes you will find that you have no thoughts there is just silence. Your body will feel heavier and relaxed allow it. This is called getting out of gravity. Once you are out of gravity fully relaxed and there is only your breathing allow yourself to hear what God is speaking to you in a state of none resistance and a nonjudgmental presumption. Allow God to guide you where He wants your thoughts to be directed towards. Listen to what He wants to say to you. Don't you lead the conversation allow God to lead the conversion. This should be done the start to the day before you get out of the bed to guide your day or at night before you go to sleep to set your intentions for the next day. It also can be done at the end of the day to create resolve and resolution your open stories of the day.

Question: Do you think you have done this because you are a smart, hardworking, likable person?

You have no boasting rights. "***God is the author*** and ***finisher of our faith***," ***Hebrews 12:2. "It is He that has made us and not we ourselves." Psalm 100:3.*** Therefore, we must always remember to acknowledge the Lord in all of our ways and He will direct our paths. Remember that God has all power and should receive all glory for your life. You are an instrument for His purpose and He needs to be able to use you for His purpose. Your purpose is His purpose. It is an assignment that was given to you before you were born. You were equipped with everything that you will need to be a success before the time clock even started for you. ***"Before I formed you in the womb I knew you, before you were born I set you apart; I appointed you as a prophet to the nations." Jeremiah 1:5***. The innate talents that you will need to accomplish your assignment cannot be taught. It can only be enhanced. You were born for the job! You were intricately created with all the right parts for God to be able to perform the work through you. God is the one that is getting it all done through you because you are a willing instrument. Make no mistake about it. Everything that you have accomplished thus far, every award, every talent you have, every business you have started, every degree you have obtain, it was not all you! You are not the miracle maker. It is the Holy Spirit that lives within us that allows us to hear from God through Christ who is our connection to God. The miracles flow through you as a result of your obedience, humility, faith, tenacity and willingness to complete the assignment.

Question: When was the last time you stop and really told God, "Thank you for all You have done."?

Every day you wake up with a gratitude prayer. Thank God for all that He has done. Starting your day in gratitude puts you in right standing with God. It automatically sets your mind in the right place. It sets the atmosphere for a blessing. It sets the room in positive energy. It set your body up in a position of surrender because you recognize that if it had not been for God you would not be here today. Gratitude prayers keep you in full recognition of who God is and how small everything is in this universe. Gratitude prayers help you to maintain humility and love for God, yourself and others.

Technique for getting your mind in the habit of praying a morning gratitude prayer

Mindfulness Technique for holding thoughts of gratitude

One technique is to sit for ten minutes and think on everything you are grateful for. This can be a challenge because it can be difficult to hold a thought for ten minutes. Start with one minute of holding on to one thought you are thankful for and then gradually increase you time of holding your thoughts.

Another technique that can help to keep you in the here and now and get your thinking under control before it takes off in its own direction is to start it out with "Thank you Lord". In the morning when you first recognize that you are awake. Start saying thank you. List off as many things you can think of off the top of your head. Lord I thank you for my eyes, ears, hands, feet, clothes, health, children, family, shoes, cars, ability to walk or talk, the trees, the house. There is no particular order of importance. It is just about thanking Him for everything and recognizing He is the one that granted all of these things we often take for granted.

It is important to start with thank you God because when you do not start here pride can easily creep in the door and cause you to stumble. Your pride will have you running in circles, your pride will make you believe that the sun rises and falls as a result of your presence.

Pride will have you walking around checking the mirror, checking your bank account and "checking" other folk. Pride is a terrible thing, but most of all pride stop purpose! The moment you begin to think that it is all you. The moment you believe that you are the reason for your success story. The moment you believe that you are the reason that things are going well. The moment you believe that you are the one that everyone needs. The moment that you believe that you bought the house, the car and started the businesses. That is the moment that YOU fail. Please hear me loud and clear on this one. Your very life depends on your ability to practice humility and live it. ***The scripture tells us in Proverbs 16:18*** Pride comes before a fall. Pride is listed on God's hate list as number one.

Bought Sense Nugget: Is Hell Real?
Some things I am not trying to be the witness on to find who is right or who is wrong.
I just take your word for it!
Auntie Diane

The worst thing you can do to quickly end your success is to start walking around saying,

"This is the house that jack built!" "I did this for you. I did that for you. You would not be where you are if it had not been for me. "I start shaking in my boots when I hear comments like that because I know there is only one way out of this comment. Down! You are going down! Your mouth has just bought you a free ticket going down! The higher up you are the harder the fall! The "I "Monster can show his ugly face in many different forms and disguises. Trust me when I tell you that you need to quickly assess him and put him down for the count. The "I "monster will have you some where laid up in a hospital, divorced, jobless, homeless, friendless, mindless. Everything stops when the "I" monster shows up! The "I" monster is the one who starts every sentences with I this or I that before they give you the list of everything that has been done. The quickest way down is to rise up. You want to go high but the way up is to stay low! Acknowledge God in all things. Recognized that it is He that has made us and not we ourselves. We are the sheep of HIS pasture! He owns the thousand cattle on the hills. The earth is the Lords and the fullness thereof. We are merely participating in His plan and being granted stewardship over His stuff.

You must understand that in order to fulfill your greatest purpose God must be at the center of all your decision and you must remember to always give Him Glory. Every sentence of appreciation should be prefaced with, "To God Be All Honor and Glory" ...then you say what you say. That statement is a reminder that whatever is about to come out of your mouth, you didn't do it. You didn't earn it. You didn't accomplish it. It was by the Grace of God that you were able to succeed in that particular race. It could have gone one hundred different ways. You could have been the one in the hospital bed, in the jail, in car accident, on the psych ward, but God! The next time you want to pat yourself on the back and tell yourself what a wonderful job you did, stop for a moment and realize that it wasn't you. We do not have bragging rights! We never will. You didn't finish the degree all by yourself. You didn't get approved for the loan all by yourself. You didn't raise those successful children all by yourself. Even if you were a single parent, trust me God sent people in your life to assist you to make sure they made it to where they were trying to go. God is so wonderful and infinite in His wisdom that He prepares a table before us before we are even old enough to eat from the table. We are often little children looking at all the fruits and cakes at the table and we never stop to recognize that we are eating from a good table. God has prepared us for where we are going and the places where we were not prepared he made a way for us. Trust God first, believe in the direction He gives you daily. Stay humble under His leadership and direction. Use all the gifts as an opportunity not to boast but to be of service. Blessings are for provisions it no more and no less. Use what God has given you to serve the people with love, compassion, caring and understanding then He will always get the glory.

Everything that God has done He has allowed it because He trusts that we can handle the responsibility of the assignment. Also it is important to recognize that as we are growing we are living from the past five to ten years of effort, knowledge, engagements, meetings, unions, strategic planning etc. God will recycle you so never think you are better than the next person. Remember, somebody showed you how to play the hand you were given. You didn't come out a genius. Someone came along and showed you your potential and pull out all the necessary parts to the equation to make you a success. God gave you a mentor, teacher or even a hard knocks life lesson to get you in place. God was trying to get you where He needed you to be to do more of His will. Depending on how you function in this cycle will determine what happens next. If you will get recycled with this hand and whatever you need to redo you redo. If you receive a new hand you will be allowed to go to the next level which includes a new set of circumstances, scenarios, people and most of all lessons. Whatever lessons you have learned you move on to the next lessons. Each cycle last about five to ten years and it is noted in your spiritual, physical, emotional and financial growth, development, stability and ability. Each new cycle creates a new financial wheel for you to work from and it runs out at the end of the cycle.

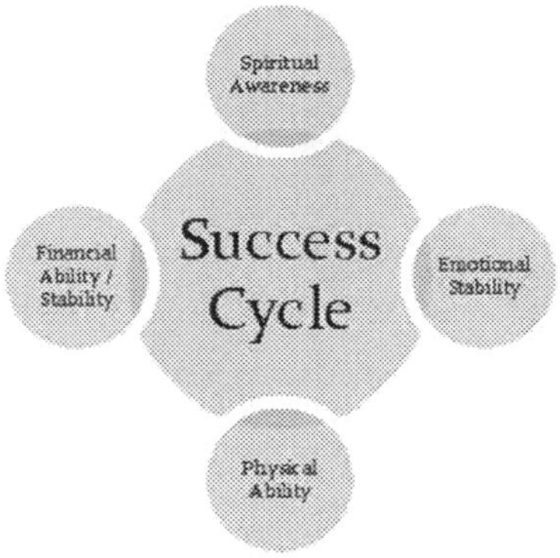

It is not difficult to see the beginning and ending of cycles. Hopefully, you have prepared to play with the upcoming deck of cards. Each hand only last about five years then you are playing a new hand which represent a new cycle. You can really see this principle in your finances. About every five to ten years you have to reinvent yourself because what worked five to ten years ago is no longer relevant or working. It has run its course and the cycle is complete. You get tired of the same old same old. You get a new boss requiring new credentials. You reserve money runs out. The job shuts down. Whatever was working last month just doesn't work anymore. That is the new hand of cards you are playing. Think about this the next time you think you have it all figured out. The new cycle is coming and you need direction from God to know what to do. You never have it under control. God is in control and He is mastering His plan through you.

Here is a technique to monitor where you are in the cycle.

I remember a time in my life when I was attending RN school. I was driving one and a half hours to school three days a week. I was in really bad marriage, sleeping in my car in the church parking lot with my children to keep peace at two am on the weekends. I had four small children, all boys under the age of ten years old. I was working sixteen hour days Tuesday, Thursday and Saturday and a full time student on Monday, Wednesday and Friday carrying 18 to 20 credit hours per semester. I had just started out and trust me the odds were definitely against me. I was determined to finish school no matter what it took. I never will forget my administrator at that time. She could see my determination to keep everything going but she also saw that I was running a rough race. She call me into her office and said, "Stacy you have a lot on your plate but I believe you can do this .You have to keep a check on yourself and know when things become too much. I do not want to ever have to come to you and pull your skirt tail to say this is too much for you. I need you to keep a wrap on yourself and maintain what is important." She went on to tell me to look at my own life and titer down where I need to titer down. The comment that stuck out the most was when she said, "Don't let me have to be the one to tell you that this is all too much." You look at yourself and everything that you are doing and tell yourself when and where it is too much. Don't make me have to evaluate your life and take things off your plate because I can see that it is too much for you. Evaluate your own life.

This is a technique that I learned during that period of my life. The way you evaluate your self is listed below

12 week evaluation of where you are in the cycle. ***If you answered yes to any of these it requires your prompt attention to make the correction for the next 12 week cycle. Do not go into the next cycle with these issues unresolved***

The four areas of your life to be evaluated every 12 weeks	Question to ask yourself	Yes No
Spiritually	Did you feel disconnected from God during anytime the past 12 weeks?	
Emotionally	Did you cuss, scream, cry, fight or want to hit someone?	
Physically	Did you physically feel sick? Did you have 5 or more days when you did not look groomed, or kept for any reason?	
Financially	Did you have any disconnect notices or threats related to your finances not being adequate?	

There is work involved in waiting. All too often people start moving around at the first sign of distress and changing their plans. Today I want to give you a new arsenal of weaponry to use when you feel frustration or anxiety. Those days when you cannot gauge what is going on and you feel as though you need to do something tell yourself these three words, "Stop! Don't Move! Remind yourself to trust God because He has it all under control. You can't understand what is going on now because it is in the middle of the process and if you move the blessing will have to reorganize itself to get to you. While you are waiting understand that the power of God is moving as a result of your words. Many times when we are going through a situation we do all the right things pray, seek counsel and immediately begin on a plan. There are times however that movement is not a good thing and you have to just wait it out. Once you have prayed, mediated and got your word from God. Wait on God to do what He said He would do. The problem is people don't know how to wait on the Lord. They wait in the wrong spirit, the wrong attitude, using the wrong words and sometimes with the wrong people. We have to always be aware that waiting still is work. ***James 1:2-8 Consider it pure joy, my brothers and sisters, [a] whenever you face trials of many kinds, 3because you know that the testing of your faith produces perseverance. 4 Let perseverance finish its work so that you may be mature and complete, not lacking anything.***

Here is a technique to keep your mind in a state of power:

While you are waiting we have a responsibility to command our own destinies through the power of our tongue but very often people have the wrong words on their tongues. It is important to put the right information in your mind so that your thinking produces the right words. The wrong thinking creates the wrong words. As you are renewing your thinking you can actively put positive words out before in the atmosphere by using I AM affirmations. I AM affirmations speak as though things already are. Instead of saying I want to be happily married. You state, "I am happily married." Instead of saying, "I want to be successful" you say I am success. Whatever it is that you would like to see in your life speak it out as though it already is and watch God assign it to you because you continue to pull it out of the atmosphere!

Write a list of I AM affirmations for yourself or simply use the list in the book. Keep it on you and say them several times throughout the day, specifically during the times when you are waiting. Use your waiting moments as an opportunity to keep your "Who I am" in the front of your subconscious mind. You must constantly renew your thinking to keep yourself thinking the right thoughts. The right thoughts are thoughts that reinforce the idea of what success looks like to you. Remember this is your idea of what you would like to have. There is no right or wrong to it. It is the desires of your heart that you are calling forward through your words. This may not involve a mission. This is a picture of what you consider success and all the items, people, places or things that your heart desires. It is your wish list.

While you are waiting to see the manifestations of greatness, trust God, use faith words, believe in the power of words and use your tongue to empower you. Only use your tongue to create positive scenarios for your day.

Here is a list of some waiting moments that people do not generally recognize:

While taking a shower have inspiration words or phrases repeating in the background.

Ironing your clothes in the morning preparing for your day have a speaker teaching you about something that is new so your mind can be engaged with the new information.

Driving in the car use audio books on subjects that interest you not necessarily about your goal or mission but other subjects too for example I love learning about different animal cycles. There is much to learn for animals because they never use words to communicate but they are constantly evolving, teaching, constructing teams, organization, hierarchy structures, and disciplinary action. You can see every form of governing in animals.

Driving the car to talk about your hopes and dreams to your children and encouraging them to also explore their hopes and dreams.

Avoid too much music. We get caught up in the storyline and the flow of music and forget about the objective which is to communicate to your subconscious all the time the direction you are going towards.

While cleaning up turn the TV off and play information in the background that reinforces the person you are trying to become.

On the phone direct the conversation to listen to what is empowering for you. Prompt the caller with ideas and thoughts that reinforce where you are going.

While cooking dinner talk to your children or loved ones about what your idea life looks like.

While you are sleeping play short audio books that last about an hour only if your mind is rested and not over stimulated.

DAILY "I AM" Affirmation

1. I AM grateful
2. I AM teachable
3. I AM lovely
4. I AM kind
5. I AM gentle
6. I AM destined for greatness
7. I AM creative
8. I AM homes
9. I AM new cars
10. I AM buildings
11. I AM refuge for the weak
12. I AM understanding
13. I AM knowledgeable
14. I AM profitable
15. I AM a wonderful spouse

16. I AM devoted to my purpose and mission
17. I AM well versed in what I am responsible for
18. I AM well in my emotions
19. I AM healthy in my thinking
20. I AM laughter
21. I AM fitness
22. I AM peaceful in my actions
23. I AM well behaved in all circumstances
24. I AM humbled everyday by God's greatness
25. I AM aware of my surrounding
26. I AM able to read the atmosphere
27. I AM quickly adaptable
28. I AM a quick study
29. I AM open to new ideas
30. I AM extraordinary
31. I AM help
32. I AM genuine
33. I AM brilliant
34. I AM healing in my land
35. I AM perfectly complete
36. I AM alert to the atmospheric changes
37. I AM in no lack
38. I AM Great in God
39. I AM abundant in every area of my life
40. I AM God's resource to work through
41. I AM full of financial resources
42. I AM a money lender
43. I AM highly favor
44. I AM provision for my family
45. I AM help for the poor and weary
46. I AM great relationship with my family
47. I AM great health
48. I AM living a long and prosperous life
49. I AM eating well

50. I AM very useful
51. I AM clear and concise in my directives
52. I AM great in communicating my needs and listening to others
53. I AM motivator
54. I AM have great relationships with people
55. I AM God anointed for the work at hand
56. I AM a prosperous person
57. I AM in great relationships in business
58. I AM able to meet my goals
59. I AM never in need for laborers
60. I AM pleased with the great service I give
61. I AM completed with my building projects
62. I AM surrounded by great leaders
63. I AM instructed by the best teachers
64. I AM counseled by the best mentors
65. I AM wearing God's Stamp of Approval
66. I AM educated in leadership
67. I AM successful in managing others
68. I AM everything I need for success
69. I AM able to have everything that I need
70. I AM a source for God to use for His purpose
71. I AM perfectly completed in God
72. I AM able to call money forth into my hand
73. I AM a healer for the land
74. I AM living in a land exclusively made for me
75. I AM fearless

Question: How do you use your influence as a leader?

We are all leaders in some area when you are in leadership position always functioning in the role of a fire preventer. When you hear the drama, use your influence to maintain the peace in the environment.

Any negativity in your environment burns up your ability to produce the positive energy you need to create. You are always creating something. Your creations are birth from a positive or negative energy forces. Minimizing drama and maintaining a peaceful environment benefit you. There are some important questions you must ask yourself before success can start to have momentum in your life. Do you defuse the drama in places where there is confrontation? Are you a fire starter or a fire preventer? Every comment that you make will either be that of a fire started or a fire preventer in the face of confrontation. **The *peacemakers are blessed, for they* will *be called sons of God. We find mercy from the Lord; may we be owned as his children, and* inherit *his kingdom Mathew 5:9***

Your positioning requires a certain level of responsibility which is a fire preventer. A fire starter is a person who sees a problem as accentuates the problems. They point out all the bad things the person is doing. They find all the weakness and put them on display. You should never use your mouth to sow seeds of discord or start fires should I say. A fire preventer unites people for the greater good, the mission, the plan, and the goals. They find the win for both sides. They find the good in every situation and in every person and accentuate it. Fire preventer see a fire brewing and they look for the extinguisher by looking for results that will allow everyone to have some level of benefit. No we will not always see eye to eye but as a leader we have a responsibility to have an open mind and at least listen to the other person. One of the quickest ways to resolve issues are to allow people to tell you how they feel. Many times they know it is wrong and they just need to hear themselves say it out loud. They will often make the corrections within themselves one way or another. They will quit the job, change the behavior or even disappear off of the scene. The fight starts when you tell the people what they are or are not going to do. One of my favorite lines is to ask a person is, "What do you think we can do to resolve this issue?" or "Tell me what you would like from me?" If I can do it then I say

I can do it but if I cannot I always tell them what I am able to do. This generally results in the person getting what they want or as close to it as I am able to give. After the fire is smothered I am able to make a decision preventing that particular fire from arising again. When I think about many of the situation that drain our time it is a direct result of a fire starter. Before a situation becomes a situation it could have gone in either direction fire or no fire. We have to decide which one we will be fire starter or fire preventer. Choose to be the person that gains momentum through peace, unity, self less service, humility, honor, respect and maintaining dignity for all people. Let God do the judging. We just need to love folk. Now that does not mean go without boundaries or limitation on what you will or will not tolerate. You should have some criteria and boundaries that are set up to contain some folk. It is important for you to know your limitation and your triggers so you do not get caught up in others people's battles. The prayer should be that the grace of God will make the changes in the person's life to help them to see themselves as God sees them. In the meantime and in between time, you should know that we are in the business of loving people and functioning as a servant. In your role as a fire fighter you should be assessing the environment and ensuring the peace is maintained so that the environment is the most conducive for successful outcomes.

Techniques to monitor your use of power

1. Ask yourself is this use of power in leadership for good or evil?
2. Does this next move minimize drama and maintain a peaceful environment?
3. Have I intensely searched for the good in this situation
4. Have I listened to the other person?
5. Have I attempted to have a reasonable compromise?
6. Have a sought out help and other listeners to have a non bias final opinion?

7. Did I take some time to really think about the outcomes for all people involved?

Bought Sense Nugget
Never let the sun go down on your anger. **Robbie Rawls**
Always seek peace by simply saying forgive me. **Robbie Rawls**

Sarah who is an affluent friend of mine had been invited to her longtime friend's birthday party. She called me after the party and was a little upset because she could see the problem with many people and why they fail to have success. She reminded me of a valuable lesson that I learned while living in Sandersville Georgia under the mentorship of one of my best friends. It has been one of the foundational pillars for the blueprint to success

Defining Moment Gauge for Elevation
Until you learn how celebrate other people's success you will never have the level of success you dream of having.
Joanne Gilbert Dotson

Here is a seemingly harmless conversation that will stop your growth and development right in its track. This is from a phone conversation:

"I was sitting at the table at the birthday party. I just came to have a good time and support a long time friend of mine and this what I encountered at one of the guest tables"

Sarah: Would you like me to bring you a piece of birthday cake?

Them: No thank you, "I don't want any."

Sarah: *(I gently smile and leave the table to get my cake. I return to the table. They evidently had been having a conversation about me while I was away.*

Them: You work at the clothing store on Virginia Beach Blvd?

Sarah: Umm, No *(I look away because I feel slightly uncomfortable)*

Them: Oh? Well, what you do?

Sarah: I work in retail for the stores in that area

Them: Girl, she owns the seventeen stores. They are everywhere. You've seen them before "The Kasual Korner". She has commercials, bill boards, everything everybody is talking about her stores. You didn't know that? Girl you so silly *(They laugh high five each other and continue their personal chatter and whispers)*

Them: Girl, that's her. Yep! Whaaatt! We were sitting next to a Ce- le- bri- ty!

Sarah*: I finish my cake and I see my good friend coming through the door and I politely excuse myself from the table. I hear them whisper as I stand up to walk away,*

Them: She thinks she's cute!

Well ladies and gentlemen she is cute and she is smart. You might as well start celebrating the fact that you were in the presence of another success story. It is important to celebrate with others as they are growing and achieving. Your ability to be genuinely happy about the success of others will be the igniting fire for your own success journey. You cannot move forward in jealously. Confrontations come from Pride. Most yelling matches happen as a result of protecting yourself and maintaining your pride. There are people who want to shine. Step back and let them. Never allow yourself to be defined by another person. Stay low stay humble and keep it moving. It is important to remember where you have come from an understanding that everyone is equal. The difference is everyone has been dealt a different card hand and everyone does not know how to play the hand they have been dealt.

Chapter Seven

Staying in the Promise land

Basic Principles
Stay on Right Course
Stay True
Stay In the loop
Stay Focus

Defining Moments Gauge for accessing your Power in God
Memory Verse
Do what is right and good in the LORD's sight, so that it may go well with you and you may go in and take over the good land the LORD promised on oath to your ancestors
Duet 6:18 (NIV)

On a Scale from 1-10 how much do I really believe this Defining Moments Scale?

0-2 Not at all (This is really hard for me to believe)
3-5 Somewhat (Sometimes I do, Sometimes I don't it just depends on the situation)
5-7 Most of the time (I live this way most days)
8-10 All the time (I live this way everyday no matter how I am feeling)

Question: How do you stay on course?

Stay on the due diligence course. It's easy to get off course. Many times people get off course because it is seems easier. It is like trying to avoid rush hour traffic. There are some things that you can't get around. You need to leave earlier, prepare yourself for what is coming so you can have an awareness of what it is going to take to get you to the other side of the road. Many times people don't want to put the time in. They do not want to do what it takes to get through the traffic to get to the final destination. They believe they can get around it. You cannot substitute time spent studying your Art. ***Study to shew* thyself approved *unto God, a workman that needeth not to be ashamed, rightly dividing the word of truth 2 Timothy 2:15*** . It may seem easier to go down another road or there may even appear to be a quicker way of getting what you need done. But at the end of the day you have to put in the time to get results.

You must also be aware that integrity is a preservative. That is some of the best advice I can give you is to do your very best to live righteous. Have right living practices. Don't intentionally do anything that you know is wrong. Practice doing the right thing all the time. Do not worry about what you need or what other people are doing and getting away with. God see's all and He knows all. Perhaps it is just a test to see if you are ready to go to the next level. Do the right thing all the time and it will keep you out of trouble. Integrity is the preservative for your life. It keeps you clean and growing.

Do not take short cuts. There is no substitute for time. There are some observations that can only be achieved through time spent working on, in, with, through the project. Some of the most important lessons that you will learn requires your hand personally spending time on. Some things you can't buy, ask, read about or even think about. You must have firsthand experience on the situation. You must see it, feel it, touch it and taste it. No one can experience it but you. YOU must put the time in! Putting the time in will fortify the integrity of the project because you personally will see to it that things are done correctly. It will have your stamp of approval on it.

I have learned to let others help me in my journey. Many times after I have surveyed the land I will and come up with the plan for the use of the land I will hand it over to my hand maidens. I allow them to work diligently on the projects to the best of their abilities. I tell them you did a great job but now I have to touch to make it work. The reason why this is important to understand is because the secret sauce to your success comes directly fromyour vision. Never fear people taking your ideas because no one can steal your vision. They can't because you have the secret sauce. It is your finger on it that is the special sauce. They may have all the paperwork needed to start the project, program or business but what they do not possess is what you have. Your DNA is what makes the vision special. It is your perspective on how it should be done. It is how you do business. It is your connection with your employees. Anyone who does not stay at your table was never supposed to be there. No matter what they do they will never be able to be like you! They can call themselves the exact same name as your dance team. The can attempt to open the exact same company as you using the same programs. It will never work! Not like you saw it working because we all view the world through a different set of lenses.

Question: How do I keep my projects alive and well?

Then after you have started your projects it is very important that you continue to blow on the flames to keep it going. You have to blow on your creation. You must personally go and blow on your dreams. In the beginning when you are creating new opportunities for success no one can blow on the creation but you. The dream is birthed from you so it has to come from the air that is in your lungs, the strength of your hands, your life force energy from your spirit and the passion of your soul. If not it won't work! Your presence creates the correct amount of energy flow to the worksite to make it happen. The machine will not even work unless you push the button. It can only be started from your fingerprints. In the beginning your hand must personally go to the plow and work the field.

As your baby grows from the newborn state into the infant role you still must be in place. People often get in trouble right here. They forget about the babies or the turn them over to people who cannot nurture them. Each mother produces a milk combination for her baby. That is not to say that the baby cannot survive on another woman's milk. The mother of the baby has specially formulated milk that is just for her babies. The milk from the mother's body is especially designed for the best possible outcomes for that particular child. Even if the mother has multiple children the milk is created for based on each child's need.

Your job is to ensure that everything you put your hand on has the ability to develop in the best possible scenario. Once it begins to crawl, you must recognize the need to watch it for danger because as we all know crawling babies get into trouble. You must be in place in order to stabilize it enough to walk steady on its own two feet before you turn it over to someone else. There is no substitute for you because it is your baby. The project is feeding off of you until it is strong enough to stand on its own. If you try to leave the project too soon it will have problems. As the project is developing you must be in place. As the projects are developing it is important for you to be in place. There are some things that only you can do. Some of the tasks may seem physically impossible for you to do. God has a way of giving us the ingenuity to figure out how to move the 7 foot cabinet to another space without getting hurt. Even if you try to get others to do the job it is still not right. The painted walls will look horrible. The cabinet won't be moved and the leak will still be coming from the roof. In the beginning when the new projects are being birth out you have to personally go talk to the roofers. You have to personally be in place to have the walls painted correctly and you may even have to get the dolly out and move the cabinet yourself. You are the only one who knows exactly what to say, how to say it, when to say it and who to say it too. You are the only one that can answer the questions behind the questions because it is your field of dreams. This is different from micromanaging. This is the work that is a requirement for the job to be a success and grow from a birth, to crawling, to walking, to running in stages of development. Once the project is up and running as we like to say. You can put people in place to maintain its operations. Until it is running expect to be in place and get it nurtured to a place of well being.

Question: How will I know when I am ready?

Due diligence equals work. Many people are not willing to invest time into them. They will not even take the time to grow their own success. Due diligence means that you have put the time in and that you have studied to master your trade. You know everything there is to know about what you are passionately pursuing. You understand and have the knowledge to work the plan. People don't want to do the work. Works equals hours of time spent laboring for pay. Due diligence is a necessary part of the journey. As you are working the dream remember there are no short cuts. Due diligence shows that you have been able to successfully focus your time, effort and energy in one area that you wish to develop long enough to gain the knowledge and expertise on working that particular plan.

The first time I heard the phrase it was you have to do your "due diligence time." I asked my friend what did that mean and she said, "You have to make and investment of time to know everything there is to know about a particular subject. You have answered all the questions from the five W's in every aspect.

Here is an example of a Due Diligence Chart. You may continue to add as many more questions that you can think of. The more questions you know the answer to the more chances that you will be able to meet you goals

Who	What	When	Where	Why
Who will be involved?	What do I need?	When do I think I can start preparing	Where will I be located	Why is this important to me?
Who will be my audience?	What will I do for the service?	When will I have enough resources?	Where will I get the resources I need?	Why is this a good time to do this?
Who will I need to accomplish my goal?	What am I trying to accomplish?	When will I need to bring in help?	Where will I find the right support systems?	Why is this important to me?
Who can support me?	What is a normal timeline for accomplishing this goal?	When can I expect to see a benefit from my work?	Where do I go to see this project or job already implemented	Why do I feel the need to do this particular thing?
Who is currently doing this?	What are the essentials of this business or goal?	When will I know I can move on to the next project?	Where are the weak areas?	Why should I invest my time effort and money in this?
Who can be my resources?	What are the pros and con's of doing this?	When will I be prepared to begin the project?	Where are the experts?	Why should anyone invest in me for this project?

Question: How do I keep from getting distracted?

Harnessing your focus is often one of the greatest challenges especially for great minded people. People become great successes because there is something is them that will not allow them to see one way of doing things. Successful people see life in color, every color of the rainbow. All the time! They hear the music. All the instruments! All the parts to include the vocals, the drum line, the piano, the horns, the strings and the drop beat all at the same time. They color the leaves in five different colors for each leaf. They couldn't see the world in black and white even if we tried. They would come up with the fifty shades of gray. When they see or hear and the opportunity to create, explore and grow they dance in the chair like a six year old child eagerly awaiting a slice of chocolate cake.

The "Dennis the Menace" behavior of exploration, pushing buttons, seeing everything as though it were the first time and not being a afraid to cross over the hole in the ground are the same tools that they must learn to harness. The same risk taking personality traits that force us to challenge our very existence everyday is the same traits that can destroy them if they do not learn to focus the energy's of our effort to produce and accomplish one goal at a time. This is the separation factor for failed success stories, mediocre success stories and great success stories. Your ability to harness your focus and maximize your efforts by putting all of your energy into one direction at a time can make you greatly successful in life, family and business.

Question: Are you on target?

We should be using a clear and concise plan of action that guides your daily actions. This is the missing link for many failed plans. The reason is because they could not harness their focus long enough to finish studying how to be a success in their trade or other areas of desire. Your ability to focus will be the deciding factor of whether or not you will be good or great. Harnessing your focus pushes you into greatness.

Each one of us should have a personal mission statement that is clear and concise that we read daily to reaffirm and help to guide our decision making processes on daily basis.

1. What is your purpose?
2. What service will you give?
3. What you expect to receive for the services that you give?

Technique for remembering to stay in a place where God can use you

<u>Staying in the promise land</u>

1. **Stay humble**- Pride comes before a fall remember it is God who has made us and not we ourselves
2. **Stay aware of your environment**- Don't get caught up in the environmental circumstances of the environment so that can stay ahead of the game. Know what you are dealing with in each day. Everyday it's a new environment, new dynamics, new energy and a new creation.
3. **Stay focus on your purpose**- When you find yourself lost go back to the basic question. What is my purpose? Why do I get up every day? What am I doing all of this for? It's not to pay the light bill. Don't let your purpose get diluted. Keep your purpose pure.
4. **Stay full of Joy** by enjoying the ride! This is a great opportunity to create a successful outcome. You win some. You lose some. It's all in the game of life. I am just happy to have an opportunity to be involved is such a great adventure!

Exercise

Write down three situations in your life that you can challenge yourself to (give up your right to be right) walk in humility. Forgive, be quiet, Don't Fight back, Sit back and let God handle it in grace and mercy.

Stop! Look around the space you are in and assess your environment.

Does it look like the person you are aspiring to become? What are you lacking?

What needs to be corrected in your environment?

Are you focused on maintaining a successful environment?

Does joy show up in your environment?

If so keep up the good work. If not, what can you fix immediately?

Spend twenty minutes a day fixing a problem, reorganizing, cleaning, following up. Fix it Today and stay in the promise land. The promise land takes work to maintain its beauty and integrity. Your job is to keep it beautiful!

Chapter Eight

Stinking Thinking

Basic Principles
Find It
Filter It
Front Load

Defining Moment gauge for your thinking
All dreams first come through your thoughts, Thoughts become Words, and Words become Beliefs. Beliefs become Reality!
Ms Cindy

On a Scale from 1-10 how much do I really believe this Defining Moments Scale?

0-2 Not at all (This is really hard for me to believe)
3-5 Somewhat (Sometimes I do, Sometimes I don't it just depends)
5-7 Most of the time (I live this way most days)
8-10 All the time (I live this way everyday no matter how I am feeling)

Question: What are you spending your time thinking about?

It is important to get rid of stinking thinking. Stinking thinking is anything that contaminates your belief process of greatness and success. It affects the way you view the world and your ability to succeed in life. People with stinking thinking view the world from the half empty cup scenario. They see all the reasons why we cannot take the land. They see every problem, deficit, potential loss or situations that could happen if. I never listen to the stinking thinkers because they always come to the table and make a mess. They sit at my dinner table with all those dirty clothes on, haven't washed their hand or even tried to wash up and it destroys the whole meal for everyone else. When they leave the table everyone appetite is spoiled because they should have never been at your table from the beginning.

The other challenge is to deal with your own stinking thinking. Everything that offends you hold be questioned. The question should be, "Why did that offend me?' If you are walking down the street and someone says, "Hey stupid!" and you turn around the question then becomes why did you turn around? What part of me believes that he was talking to me? Why did I identify myself as being stupid? You have to decide. You have to choose. You have to proclaim who you are and in your mind be that person even before it is manifested in your life. Things happen so quickly in the atmosphere that it takes time for it to manifest itself. Every day you speak a new existence into your script of life. All of your thoughts must align themselves with who you hope to be. It is important to allow yourself to think about your future self. Who do I think I would like to become. The wonderful part about this is you do not have to be right. It does not have to be perfect you just need to begin to develop who you would like to become.

Defining Moments
Your mind is like your closet.
If you want to know how your state of mind is look in your closet! **Uncle Damon**

Question: What do I hear garbage or gold?

We have over 70,000 thoughts per day. So our minds have learned to filter information out so that we do not get bombarded with information overload. We gather information in two fundamental areas and we view it as Garbage or Gold. Garbage represents anything that does not build you up. Garbage creates feelings of unworthiness, sadness, remorse, regret and jealousy. Gold fortifies and strengthens you for your journey. Gold is precious information that will help to establish your thinking patterns and the behaviors associated with moving you towards your goals.

We go through life on a scavenger hunt for gathering information that will make our lives better. We look for people, things, situations, and circumstances that will make us feel better physically, spiritually and emotionally. So throughout the day we are constantly making decision about what words, people, thoughts and circumstances are garbage or gold. The question is what conversations, people, circumstances, comments and thoughts are you allowing yourself to take in and how is the information stored. You make information gathering decisions everyday all day. All questions are shelved in two places based on whether or not we view it as garbage or gold. This then becomes your filter system for making decisions. Before we allow the information to come into the storage parts of our brains we ask ourselves two questions: Is this garbage or gold? Is this information good for me or is this information bad for me? We shelf the information somewhere under garbage or gold and we use that information to make the decisions. Those decisions ultimately determine our destinies.

Think about what your are allowing to come through your filters. You do not have to expose yourself to everything. Make quick assessments on whether or not you should even allow certain information to go past your first glance.

1. What are you allowing yourself to be exposed to and why?
2. What are you storing certain information?
3. What are you dumping immediately?
4. If you are storing garbage, why?

Memory Verse
Philippians 4:8 (KJV)
Finally, brethren, whatsoever things are true, whatsoever things are honest, whatsoever things are just, whatsoever things are pure, whatsoever things are lovely, whatsoever things are of good report; if there be any virtue, and if there be any praise, think on these things.

Question: How do you see the world?

Your perception of how you interpret the information will determine where you place the information in your value system. Your perception equals your world view. It is the lens in which you see the world. Whatever lens you are viewing the world from will determine where you place the new information you learned. It will determine how you will project your thoughts into the world. The half empty cup versus half full cup is how we view the world. The problem with negative perception is that when you gather information and it is filtered from a place where your basic needs are not met or threaten your decision making process get contaminated. Decision making should never be made from a place of Emergency or Urgency. When a decision is made based on an emergency or urgent need the decision making process filter gets clogged up and we need a filter change. Never make decision from desperation. God will handle everything that you need. If you are feeling anxious and desperate it is important to think before you act. Use a relaxation technique that allows you to lie down and relax so that God can show you His plan.

Technique to monitor your thoughts

Each morning you should listen to audio tapes that reinforce value thoughts. Use tapes to condition your mind into the thoughts that will add value for today's assignment. If you need skills in getting organized listen to audio tapes while you are doing task that do not require your attention for example: folding clothes, getting dressed, bathing, combing your hair etc.

These are the activities that we do on "Autopilot". When you are doing these activities this is the best time to do the thought pushing techniques. When you do not have something that you are directing your thoughts towards your thoughts will direct you.

We must constantly get in front of our thinking and direct our thoughts in the direction we want to move in. Your thoughts produce an energy that will move in a particular direction. Where ever you are standing, sitting, lying at this very moment is because your thoughts directed you to be in that place. Every day we have to consciously direct our thoughts into the direction we are expecting to have a change in. If you are traveling towards wealth then play wealth audio tapes. If you are traveling towards weight loss then you must play, read and talk about weight loss. If you are traveling towards positive relationships then play, read and talk about how make relationships positive.

Chapter Nine

Refuse to Die!

Basic Principles
Burn the Ship
Build the dream
Believe Failure is not an option

Defining Moments for gauging your Tenacity -If the ship goes down somewhere in the middle of the ocean... come looking for me because I will be somewhere floating on a piece of wood.
Robbie Rawls

On a Scale from 1-10 how much do I really believe this Defining Moments Scale?

- 0-2 Not at all (This is really hard for me to believe)
- 3-5 Somewhat (Sometimes I do, Sometimes I don't it just depends)
- 5-7 Most of the time (I live this way most days)
- 8-10 All the time (I live this way everyday no matter how I am feeling)

Question: What will it take for you to refuse to go back?

Burn the ship up when you get across the shore line. Too often people give themselves an option to go back. Once you make up in your mind that you cannot return to your old way of doing business the rest is history. The day you wake up and decide that you are burning the boat is a good day because that is the day the world will see what fabric you are truly cut from. It is the day you say to yourself, "I will not give myself the option to return back to where I came from. This is the day that I will see if I can fly or if I have to be rescued but this is the day I will truly know if I can fly. I am Peter Pan. I say I am Peter Pan so I can fly. If you don't believe me just watch me! The boat is burned up and here I stand!

There are not enough times that we allow our bags of tenacity and perseverance to be tapped into. When we become afraid of failure and the unknown that is when we retreat to what we know. I believe that a natural part of your growing process require a sense no return to the old way. Those are the times when we burn the boat up and start a new life. No use in looking back because you can never go back there you have purposely discarded all the resources, people, situations, even those things you may have thought had some level of value you release into the atmosphere with a prayer of it returning to you if you are supposed to have it. God is infinite in His wisdom. He knows what we have need of everyday. He will protect us, He will lead us and He will guide us for His greater purpose. We have to learn how to quickly assess when it is time to burn the boat once we make it to the new shore.

Once the boat is burn there is no going back! It keeps you looking towards your future with expectation because you realize that you do not have anything to go back to. You must succeed on this side of the fence. You must learn how to sustain yourself off of these new resources. You must learn how to use these new tools. You must learn how to walk differently, talk differently. You must learn everything you need to be a success over here. The boat is burned up and you can't leave this side anymore if you tried. So you might as well get busy working over on this side of the shore line.

On this side of the shore line you start building a new dream. The tools you need to build this dream can only be found in this place. The tools you had before do not fit. They do not work. There is a different level of responsibility, authority, power and influence that is required on this side of the shoreline. So it is important to learn everything you need to know on this side of the shore. As you grow there will be people, behaviors, thought patterns and habits you cannot take with you to the other side. God has assigned each one of us according to our faith a measure of wholeness. ***According to your faith, thy faith hath made the whole. Mark 5:34***

Then there are levels of authority given to us. There are levels of authority that each person has assigned to their lives and it is based their growth and development in the four pillars of evaluation: spiritual, emotional, physical and financial. Every time you get a spiritual promotion it comes with greater responsibilities and more people will be affected by the decisions that you make. New levels of commitment require information that allows you to be able to function in this capacity. It also creates the new devils that you have to make sure you keep at bay and under control. The new levels create new responsibilities. You move into greater positions of authority based on the people's belief that you know how to fix the problem. You become the decision maker for your families, your business and even your communities. Thank God, it is not all on you. God has a way of blessing us with the cup that we need to drink from to maintain our strength and give us the wisdom to deal the current level of responsibility. After you have been qualified to be in the positions of authority God also gives us a cup of New Mercies that will be available to sustain us in our weakness. ***His grace is***

sufficient to supply all of my needs according to His riches and glory. (Philippians 4:19)

Question: Do you know that you know that everything is going to work out for your good?

When you act as THOUGH and not as IF, your true destiny will manifest in a timely manner. The people who act as THOUGH function everyday as though they already are who they are dreaming of becoming. They walk around with a presence that says I am a millionaire, a doctor, a teacher, a nurse, a wife, a mother long before it manifest itself. They already start preparing themselves to take on the roles and responsibilities of the position that are requesting. They learn the language and live a lifestyle the reaffirms their ideas of the persons that they envision themselves to become in their future. They act as though they already are that person by making decision and living a standard of life that is in alignment with who they say they will become. The decision making process in based from a place of believing they already have what they desire. Many times before the reality can take place you have to go through the process of change in your thinking to get there. People who act as though don't mind going through the process because they have been living in that capacity in a mindset for so long that they are already accustom to the lifestyle. The lifestyle will catch up to mentality. The mentality comes first and they lifestyle will manifest itself as quickly as you can believe it will manifest itself.

People who act as if function from the "If factor" They view everything from the perspective of fear of something happening. Fear stops faith! Every time fear and disbelief enter into your thinking it halts that progress of your success. Every time you build an idea from the presence of If i.e. fear you cannot move forward until you get pass the what if's. Instead of building a project, a dream, a relationship, a house from the "what if" factor, build it in the right place, with the right person, on the right principles and with the right motives in place. We can never predict the future all we can do is ***Seek ye first the Kingdom of God and all of His righteousness Math 6:33,*** then trust God's direction, live right one day at a time and do the best we can to responsibly serve people with the resources will have been given. When we learn this concept the if factor becomes void because we can trust that everything we need will come due to our seeking God's direction, living right and believing God for everything that we need.

Question: What if I do everything right and I still fail?

Failure is never failure it is merely direction. God has sent pointers in your life to help to guide and direct your steps. God will allow encounters with people, situations and circumstances to move you into the direction that you need to be headed towards for his purpose. Those situations that seem like failures are a part of the plan for your success. It had to happen. It was a "Must Needs go through place." How many times have you ever said, "I will never do that again!" and you really believed you would not do it but you found yourself doing it again. Then there were the times when you said, "I will never do that again!" and you never did it again. What was the difference? I want to suggest that you got it that time. You shelved the information in the right part of your brain and it reminded you of the cost verse the benefit. The cost was too much and the benefit was too little. You learned how to adapt to the environment to preserve yourself from the discomfort associated with that particular loss. When there is loss, more cost and less benefit change occurs. Failure helps change to occur. We learn how to adjust based on previously learned information. Failure does not equal defeat. Failure equals direction.

Question: What about the days when I just cannot take anymore, then what?

You may think that you are down for the count but hold on! Some days you may feel as though you cannot take another day of the life you are currently living. Sometimes you may feel as though everything around you is falling down and the very ground you walk on is crumbling with every step you take. You may feel as though you have fought your last fight and gave everything you could give. You don't have another tear to cry. Hold on and trust that help is on the way! God has already dispatched chariots of angels that are coming to war on your behalf. Keep your battle gear on and hold your head up in the fight. Keep your word locked and loaded with faith. Don't you bow and don't you bend. God has already made a way for you if you just trust Him. My brothers and my sisters hold on to your dreams. Hold on to your hope. Hold on to memories of everything that God has already done in the past to prove His presence is real. Hold on in a position of thanksgiving. While you are holding on, keep fighting, keep breathing, keep believing, keep encouraging yourself, keep living, today is not the day to give up. Hold on tight and don't let go! Never give up and never give in!

Bought Sense Nuggets:
Find the strength to find your way...The Calvary ain't coming!
But God will be there
Auntie Stacy
If you want to quit remind yourself why you started....**Charity**

Chapter Ten

A Good Steward over Everything

Basic Principle Money Talk Money Responsibility Money Management	<u>**Defining Moment on gauging how you handle money**</u> *"Money doesn't change people it only enhances who you already are"* **Ms Cindy**

On a Scale from 1-10 how much do I really believe this Defining Moments Scale?

0-2 Not at all (This is really hard for me to believe)
3-5 Somewhat (Sometimes I do, Sometimes I don't it just depends)
5-7 Most of the time (I live this way most days)
8-10 All the time (I live this way everyday no matter how I am feeling)

Question: Are you ready to talk money?

As you grow in trusting God, money will become the least of your concerns. This is the last thing that you need. Money is everywhere and those who understand this concept never have a problem neither getting money nor keeping money. It is the people who work from a spirit of scarcity that will never have enough of it. The problem is they do not understand that money represents responsibility, accountability and reliability. For people who have money, it is the last thing they discuss. They talk about character traits like consistency, honesty, passion, what you understand about your where you are trying to go, your success stories, your failure stories, your circle of influence, your past five years and none of these questions have a right or wrong answer.

Question: Are you ready to handle the responsibilities of success?

The first rule for understanding money is that destiny calls provision forward therefore you never have to depend on the money system in this world to move forward in your Destiny. Your destiny is not predicated on your current resources. Your destiny is always built on future resources. Every resource, every person, and every little thing that you need will be provided for you as you walk through your journey. Do not allow the visual lack of resources, finances or even people to stop you from walking in your destiny. You will have everything you need provided for you while you are on the journey. Destiny calls you towards everything you need. You mouth creates your destiny. You call forth the very existence of what you need.

Secondly, Poverty is not about money. Poverty is a mindset. Poor thinking create stagnate living. Poor thinking causes you to live from an idea of scarcity. You do not believe you will have enough so you refuse to give up what you can currently see. You hold onto a job or situation that will allow you to maintain a particular benefit whether it is called a disability check, a housing voucher, a food voucher, a man or a position at work. It doesn't matter how you wrap it. It is all the same. You refuse to give up what you currently have because you do not believe that there is a better house, job, relationship, paycheck, position. You are scared to give up what you have. I have seen it time and time again. People actually say, "I cannot make more than this amount of money because I will lose my check, my section 8 voucher, my daycare, my disability check and the list goes on. If you just get out here and start it will be enough to take care of all of those needs and the "benefits" won't matter. This is one of the hardest lessons to teach because it is a mindset that needs to be destroyed. Thoughts become things! If you have a poverty mentality then you will have a poverty lifestyle.

Memory Verse
Proverbs 23:7 King James Version (KJV)
For as he thinketh in his heart, so is he: Eat and drink, saith he to thee; but his heart is not with thee.

You can pay your bills by yourself! You can eat without assistance! You can make it! You have to believe that God is a provider and start moving along your journey in freedom, abundance and expectation of your needs and desires manifesting today. God will provide. He is a provider. Either you get this part of the story or you don't. Trust me this is an important part of the story so you need to get it!

Question: Outside of your family, who will you serve with the provision that God gives you?

Finally, when God gives us a gift it should be pour back into the people. The more provision you need the more will be provided. It still amazes me when I see God moving and allowing the universe to pour itself resources into my ideas. God provides everything we need. He loves so much and He desires for us to love one another, compassionately and concerned. God provides for us for the purpose of helping one another. We are to serve, give, love, respect, teach, and care. That why God provides. Either you get this part or you don't. Trust me this is important to understand.

Exercise

Purchase a journal and several poster boards to create your life

Vision Board and Dream Journals are tools to help you began to manifest your dreams

Take the time to cut out pictures of everything you imagine your life to be, fill up your entire poster board with pictures of what you want your life to look like. Make sure there is no white space left on the board. Post it in your bedroom so you can see it every day. Watch what will happen over the next ninety days. As your vision board manifests itself you will find that your energy will become scattered as the board is completing itself. Be prepared to have your second vision board ready as the first one is closing out. Whenever I feel scattered and all over the place, I know that everything that was on my vision board is just about complete and my energy does not have a direction. I have to create a new board to give my energy direction.

Dream Journals are also good to write out because they allow you to write out your vision in detail. It is also good because you go back a read where God has brought you from.

It is important to think on whatsoever things are just, lovely, kind and beautiful because those are the things that you get. As I think about my life and where I want to be it is always a lovely place full of kindness and beauty. As I focus my thoughts on the things that are pure, kind lovely and beautiful those are the things that I receive. I encourage you to dream regularly about the home, family, marriage, job, business, church family and anything else that will make you happy. It is only through your dreaming that the birth of greatest can be conceived. Wealth is a mentality that first starts in your mind.

Mindfulness Technique

Take about five to ten minutes a day to allow yourself to explore in detail what it would feel like to have everything that is in your dreams.

Choose one thing on your board or in your dream journal

Get a piece of your favorite candy; make sure it is in the wrapper when you start this exercise

Use your eyes to SEE IT (Look at all the parts of it)

Use your ears to HEAR IT (What does it sound like as you are opening it?)

Use your nose to SMELL IT (What does it smell like?)

Use your hands to FEEL IT (What does it feel like on your tongue before you bite into it, once you bite into what does it feel like once you bite into it, how does it feel in your teeth, on your tongue?)

Use your tongue to TASTE IT (As you are chewing it, take your time to allow yourself to taste flavors, after it is gone what do you taste)

(You probably want to do this alone or in a group of people all doing the exercise.)

I realize this sounds a little different so use a piece of candy to understand the concept of this mindfulness technique. What is does is allows your mind to be in the here and now. It helps you to really enjoy the moment. This one moment in time I am going to stop everything and see it, smell it, taste it, feel it. This is a wonderful relaxation technique that also helps to clear your thinking. If you learn how to focus on enjoying a piece of chocolate candy it can really produce a significant pleasure moment. Try it out! The goal is to clear your mind and allow yourself to be able to concentrate on one thing at a time to fully enjoy that moment. The goal here is to learn how to clear your mind, focus on one thing, and be in the here and now of your moment.

Question: Are you prepared to handle great wealth?

Matthew 25:14-30English Standard Version (ESV)
The Parable of the Talents

14 *"For it will be like a man going on a journey, who called his servants[a] and entrusted to them his property.*
15 *To one he gave five talents,[b] to another two, to another one, to each according to his ability. Then he went away.*
16 *He who had received the five talents went at once and traded with them, and he made five talents more.*
17 *So also*

he who had the two talents made two talents more. [18] *But he who had received the one talent went and dug in the ground and hid his master's money.* [19] *Now after a long time the master of those servants came and settled accounts with them.* [20] *And he who had received the five talents came forward, bringing five talents more, saying, 'Master, you delivered to me five talents; here I have made five talents more.'* [21] *His master said to him, 'Well done, good and faithful servant.*[c] *You have been faithful over a little; I will set you over much. Enter into the joy of your master.'* [22] *And he also who had the two talents came forward, saying, 'Master, you delivered to me two talents; here I have made two talents more.'* [23] *His master said to him, 'Well done, good and faithful servant. You have been faithful over a little; I will set you over much. Enter into the joy of your master.'* [24] *He also who had received the one talent came forward, saying, 'Master, I knew you to be a hard man, reaping where you did not sow, and gathering where you scattered no seed,* [25] *so I was afraid, and I went and hid your talent in the ground. Here you have what is yours.'* [26] *But his master answered him, 'You wicked and slothful servant! You knew that I reap where I have not sown and gather where I scattered no seed?* [27] *Then you ought to have invested my money with the bankers, and at my coming I should have received what was my own with interest.* [28] *So take the talent from him and give it to him who has the ten talents.* [29] *For to everyone who has will more be given, and he will have an abundance. But from the one who has not, even what he has will be taken away.* [30] *And cast the worthless servant into the outer darkness.*

Question: What do I do to get out of my financial mess?

Don't act deep when it comes to money! Do the right thing. One of the lessons I had to learn early on was to Render Caesar what belongs to Caesar and give God what belongs to God. Don't give away your rent money and expect not to get an eviction notice. Pay your bills on time. Call your creditors and make arrangement to get out of your mess. Only buy what you can pay for based on your own income. Never spend from other people's pocket. Spend from your resources because those are the only resources you can truly control. It is a wonderful idea to have two people on the same team with the same goals, moral compasses and spending habits but for the most part it doesn't happen. So only make purchase that you personally can guarantee. This is not a prayer thing. It is not spiritual. It is common sense. What kind of foolishness is it for you to commit to a mortgage of $2200 dollars a month because the lender said based on you and your husband's income you were eligible for this amount of mortgage over the next thirty years. You should be saying, "What?!" No, thank you how much house can we get on one income in fifteen years. Why get that kind of debt and have to pray every month to pay the mortgage. Foolishness I say, FOOLISHNESS. Pay cash for as many items in your home as you can pay. No one should be able to take stuff back from you. Buy what your money will allow you to buy during this season of your life. If you manage the resources you have today. God will bless you with more tomorrow.

Question: How do I tithe when I cannot even pay the bill I have now?

Many times when people come into the church one of the first lessons they learns about is tithing and offering Yes they are both important and I believe in both. What I have found to be the greatest challenge is the transitional period from being over committed and under paid and trying to balance your commitment to God and pay off all these people you owe. What do you do? Pray and ask God to give you the wisdom on how to get out of the mess and give your offering faithfully. ***As you are growing in God's grace, knowledge and faith in Him providing start tithing.*** The tithing principle is a faith principle. If you do not believe that God will provide for you as you are tithing it will not work. You must believe that

God is your provider. God will prove Himself to you as you grow in your understanding and knowledge of Him. God knows your heart and He knows what your intentions. There will come a time when you have paid all the people you owe and you are moving in a faith realm that allows you to believe God for the supply but until then keep building your faith, giving your offering and paying your bills. Always make every attempt to pay people on time. Don't over commit. If you tell someone you are going to pay them then pay them. Stop using excuses as to why you cannot pay a person what you owe. If you owe, you owe! Stop getting into commitments with people and you won't have to spend the resources you have been given. Remember money is a resource for a service you have been provided. Perhaps one should not require so many services to be rendered and you could have a little extra in your pocket!

Question: Why don't I have enough money no matter how much I work?

Lack of money can become a financial issues are because people do not understand the principle of money. Money is everywhere and it is constantly flowing to somewhere. It flows in and it flows out that is why money is called currency. It should flow from one place to another to meet needs by providing a service. If money is at a standstill in your life it is because you do not allow it to flow freely to and from the right places. People who have money issues have them because they don't understand money flows where there is a need. Money flows to the people who understand it and know what to do with it when they get it. When I look at people with money issues, the first questions I ask them is how much does your cell phone bill cost? How often do you eat out? Is your car clean? Did you make your bed today? These questions are all indicative of stewardship, responsibility, commitment and care of what they currently have. If you do not even care enough to make your bed in the morning and clean the car that your drive everyday then why should you receive finances to get more stuff that you do not take care of. Money will flow where there is a need. Trust me we do not live in a society, world, universe, that is foolish to pour itself into places with no return. You do not have enough because at this current moment you do have enough! Manage what you currently have first. Money flows where it needs to go.

If you take all of money out of the richest people's hand and give it to all the rest of the world within five years they will have it all back because they understand how to use money. Their spending habits are different from people who do not have money. People who have money have practices of handling money that is different from people who do not have money. The respect level for money is different. It is not that they love money. It is an understanding of how to use money. They understand the word currency and the flow in which money should be used.

Question: How do I know I am ready to handle more money?

The greater the amount of the weight that your project will carry the greater the amount of responsibility you will carry. God gives us resources based on our ability to handle the fiscal responsibility, the ethical responsibility, the moral responsibility, the legal responsibility, the spiritual responsibility and even the physical and emotional responsibility. Handling money is not a joke! If someone hands you money they expect something in return. Money is given in exchange for a service that you will be ultimately responsible for providing. The more money you are given the greater the level of responsibility you are given and it is not just in providing services. It includes higher level of character responsibility. The financial resources that God makes available to you are in direct proportional relationship to the level of responsibility for services you will provide.

For each level of understanding you must first understand what you are doing. The money comes as a result of your understanding. The money comes as you show you are responsible for using and maintaining the checks and balances system to insure that you are maintaining accountability. God will provide you with the resources to accommodate you for the amount of services that you will oversee. The more understanding of the responsibility plus the understanding of HOW to be accountable at this level of responsibility equals the financial resources that will be given to you. ***Wisdom is the principal thing; therefore get wisdom: and* with all thy getting get understanding (Proverbs 4:7)**

Responsibility for Services + Level of Understanding = Financial Resources

(Divided By)

Maintaining accountability

Thus greater finances will come with you level of understanding of the responsibility you have been assigned and the ability to be accountable for the resources.

Access to wealth creates a need for fiscal responsibility. God has provided many resources through people. You will only be exposed to the amount of resources for the amount of your dream. Is your dream big enough to be a part of these kinds of conversations? What are you talking about during the time allotted to you? What are planning? What are working on? What contributions are you making to society? What do you need? All that is required is for you to dream big enough, and then have the correct conversation to seal the assignment therefore calling forth all the resources needed to produce the results.

2 Kings 4New International Version (NIV)
The Widow's Olive Oil

4 The wife of a man from the company of the prophets cried out to Elisha, "Your servant my husband is dead, and you know that he revered the Lord. But now his creditor is coming to take my two boys as his slaves."

2 Elisha replied to her, "How can I help you? Tell me, what do you have in your house?"

"Your servant has nothing there at all," she said, "except a small jar of olive oil."

3 Elisha said, "Go around and ask all your neighbors for empty jars. Don't ask for just a few. 4 Then go inside and shut the door behind you and your sons. Pour oil into all the jars, and as each is filled, put it to one side."

5 She left him and shut the door behind her and her sons. They brought the jars to her and she kept pouring. 6 When all the jars were full, she said to her son, "Bring me another one."

But he replied, "There is not a jar left." Then the oil stopped flowing.

7 She went and told the man of God, and he said, "Go, sell the oil and pay your debts. You and your sons can live on what is left."

Work as though you have every resource to do what needs to be done. When I work in this manner I have found that I ran out of pots. God provides all the resources that I need. Many times, I run out of ideas and I have to go back to the drawing board and create new dreams because they have all been fulfilled.

Question: How should I spend the money?

Never eat your seed. You should only be eating from the fruit of your labor. It is a foolish man who eats his seed. Money that is given to you to help you get on your feet represents seed. Money that you had to borrow due to hard times represents seed. Money that is given to help you get started on a project represents seed. Never take money from these places they are your seed. If you use the seed money correctly it will produce the fruit of your labor. If you use the seed correctly it can be used to plant in more fields to help more people. A seed is planted every time we pay on a long term bill, start a business or fund a new project. Do the seeds you are planting produce fruit? Seeds are the places where you are investing your time. What do you get from the time and money you spend? Is there a portion of your money always used for seed planting? You should be eating from the fruit. What is produce as a result of your efforts? What do you have a result of the time, effort and energy you have given?

Matthew 14:13-21New International Version (NIV)

Jesus Feeds the Five Thousand

13 When Jesus heard what had happened, he withdrew by boat
privately to a solitary place. Hearing of this, the crowds followed
him on foot from the towns. 14 When Jesus landed and saw a large
crowd, he had compassion on them and healed their sick.

15 As evening approached, the disciples came to him and said, "This is a remote place, and it's already getting late. Send the crowds away, so they can go to the villages and buy themselves some food."

16 Jesus replied, "They do not need to go away. You give them something to eat."

[17] "We have here only five loaves of bread and two fish," they answered.

[18] "Bring them here to me," he said. [19] And he directed the people to
sit down on the grass. Taking the five loaves and the two fish and
looking up to heaven, he gave thanks and broke the loaves. Then
he gave them to the disciples, and the disciples gave them to the
people. [20] They all ate and were satisfied, and the disciples picked up
twelve basketfuls of broken pieces that were left over. [21] The number
of those who ate was about five thousand men, besides women and
children.

Question: How do I keep from getting burned out?

Take the time to say, "What a great job! To God be all glory!" Sometimes we brush pass our successes so fast that we never stop to enjoy the beauty of the success. Success should be celebrated! We have spent years getting to a place of self fulfillment and often we don't take two seconds to stop and look at it. Allowing yourself to have great days and taking appropriate amount of time to celebrate your accomplishments is a good thing and it helps to fuel us for the next goal as well as gives us a stopping and starting point to measure our success from. For the overachiever it is often challenging to allow yourself a moment to say that you have been blessed. It is okay to look over the accomplishment and take in the beauty of the success while acknowledging that God the Father is the miracle maker and we are His tools. We should see the glory of God upon our lives and have a story to tell as a result of God's love, grace, mercy and provision.

Defining Moments gauge to finishing task
If you believed that the project was good enough to start then it is good enough to finish!
Ms Cindy

Question: What is your Great Work!

God has begun a great work in you and He will finish it. Trust in the opportunities that God gives you and believe in the power given to us from resurrection of Jesus Christ. ***For God has not given us a Spirit of Fear but of Power, Love and Self Discipline 2Tim 1:7*** which is everything you need to fuel your daily bread promises and renew your strength, acts of kindness and commitment to finish what has been started. You have been assigned a great work. We all have. Once I believed that the great work was only for a few chosen people but we have all commissioned to set the captives free, destroy the yokes of bondage and do the great work of helping people to have a greater understanding of who the Father is while gaining a personal relationship with him as well as partaking in an abundant life. There are many people depending on your success each one of us have a role to play in this world. There are no big I's and little you. We all have value and purpose. The fact that you are reading this book means that you are on your way. Things bother you that don't affect other people. You have a need to make a change and be the change. You are at critical level most days as you go through your day. It is a challenge for you to act normal, get a job, go home and watch TV like the rest of the world. I understand and that is why I write to encourage you and help you to write a new story for generations to come. You are a trailblazer. You were born for this level of intensity. You can stand it. You can do it. God has equipped you and create you in a wonderful fashion. God built you for this stuff. Allow God to lead you on your mission and allow Him to give you all the resources, people, energy and supply that you need to accomplish your Great Work!

Conclusion of the Matter: How Bad Do You Want It?

People can tell you many things. Everyone has a quick fix one, two, three, steps to success method. The question is: How bad do you want it? There is always a subject matter expert to help you to get to where you are trying to go. You can have all of the answers to the test given to you but if you refuse to study and do not put the time in you will fail. Success will only come when we come to a place where we are sick and tired of being sick and tired. The day you wake up and recognize that you are your only problem. It is not your brother, your sister, your mother or the people that cause you not to soar. Your wings are not strengthen because you have refused to spread them and attempted to fly with your own two wings. You have not attempted to stand on your own two feet. You have not attempted to trust God in your own situation. You have not opened your heart and mind to trust God for your own life. How bad do you want it? How bad do you need it? Have you said ENOUGH! I will have a better way of living my life and it will start today!

I also want to appeal to those who saying, "I have done all I can and it is still not working". You have believed. You have been in the presence of God. You have continued to do the work of the Lord. You go to church on Sundays and Wednesdays, paid your tithes, read your bible and done all the things you have been taught however you are still not where you want to be in life. I want to challenge you to allow your faith to come alive and receive His blessings. God has a plan for your life. We have to run into the blessing. Lean into the painful places, Go into the blind spaces even when we do not understand what is going on. You are the hold up! How bad do you want it! I challenge you to GO!

I speak over those who have inherited a debt that doesn't belong to you. This is a debt that was acquired long before you were born. You have been handed a long list of junk that you didn't have anything to do with. It seems as though you are paying a penalty from being born in the rough situation. I want to encourage you because you may not have been given the tools you need to become a success. Most of you really do want it bad but there is no one to show you how to get it. God has spoke over your very existence today and you are released from every chain, every generational curse, every moment that attempts to cripple your walk, every circumstance the enemy has set before you. I bind the hand of the enemy over your life. I release God's grace and mercy over your life. I release the anointing to destroy every yoke assigned to your life. I bind every hindering spirit, every frustrating spirit, every antagonizing spirit, every demonic spirit assigned to your life. I cast it back to the pit of Hell and I release God's ministering angels to do the assignment God has given them in agreement with your destiny. I release a mind that allows the Holy Spirit to teach you all things. God is greater than your past and He is going to work it all out for your good. Reach up and reach out because the blessings are at your finger tips.

And finally I want to touch the blind man. If you are the skeptic, the one who is thinking that this stuff was a good read but I am not sold on it. You are not convinced that by applying these principles with God as the center of your direction you will have success. You have read the entire book but yet it is hard to buy into the concepts of your words having power and your mind needing silence so you can hear and your circles being extremely important. I want to speak to your blindness today. I spent many years in the darkness. I was blind, ignorant, arrogant and downright foolish but it took God to send people in my life to help me to see what was right in front of me. My life was a train wreck. I had been married twice with four children by the time I was twenty three. I had so much foolishness going on that it was a norm for me. I didn't understand what it felt like not to live crazy. I was living in a dark place and did not know it. I was afraid to be alone so I got into horrible relationships that cost me dearly. I didn't know who I was. I didn't know where I was going. I hated my life. I felt all alone yet I was surrounded by people who loved me. I was seated at a table of regret, chaos and foolery BUT God kept me. I want you to know that you can stand up from that table and begin a new life today. Stand up and shout onto the Lord. Shout victory and run into your new life. Your destiny is not where you are currently seated. Your destiny awaits you. Today, I call you to your new seat. Come sit among kings and queen. Rest your feet at the table of royalty. You are Royal! You are a child of the King. I proclaim that your crying days from foolishness are over. I proclaim that you will see. You will have understanding. You will use the principles of success to move you to the right table and stabilize your life so you can grow on a solid God centered foundation. God created to live a life that was full of abundance. He has given you everything you need all you have to do is call it forward, believe Him, trust Him even though you cannot see. You must know that no matter what God will never leave you nor forsake you. He is our God and He wants us to live a successful life as Kings and Queens that are joint heir of the Most High God!

So dry your eyes and wipe your face
Step up my kings and queens and take your place.
You are queens and kings and shall always be
For God has already set you free

God bless you and I love you dearly!

Reference Page

Covey's Time Management Quadrants-Stephen Covey 7 Habits of highly effective People

Doran, G, Management Review, S.M.A.R.T *retrieved 12/02/2017*

King James Bible

New International Version

Printed in the United States
By Bookmasters